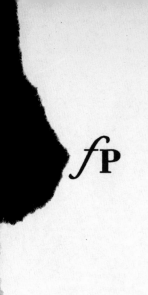

Also by Ron Willingham

Integrity Selling for the 21st Century
The People Principle
Hey, I'm the Customer
When Good Isn't Good Enough
Integrity Selling
The Best Seller

Integrity Service

Treat Your Customers Right—

Watch Your Business Grow

Ron Willingham

Free Press

New York   London   Toronto   Sydney

FREE PRESS
A Division of Simon & Schuster, Inc.
1230 Avenue of the Americas
New York, NY 10020

Copyright © 2005 by Ron Willingham
All rights reserved,
including the right of reproduction
in whole or in part in any form.

FREE PRESS and colophon are trademarks of Simon & Schuster, Inc.

For information regarding special discounts for bulk purchases,
please contact Simon & Schuster Special Sales at 1-800-456-6798
or business@simonandschuster.com

Designed by Jeanette Olender
Manufactured in the United States of America

10 9 8 7 6 5 4 3 2 1

Library of Congress Cataloging-in-Publication Data
Willingham, Ron, 1932–
     Integrity service : treat your customers right, watch your business grow /
Ron Willingham.
        p. cm.
     1. Customer services. I. Title.
HF5415.5.W585   2005
658.8'12—dc22   2005040870

ISBN-13 978-0-7432-7027-4
ISBN-10 0-7432-7027-4

Trademark permissions copy appears on page 267.

To Bernard Petty . . .

Friend, business partner, and person who only saw

the best in me. Who could ask for anything more?

Special Thanks . . .

To Dianna Melson, Sarah Bryan, and Robin Willingham

for your hours of typing manuscripts, redoing my

revisions, and redoing my revisions.

To super agents Jane Dystel and Miriam Goderich—

you couldn't have been more helpful than you were.

To my Simon & Schuster editor Fred Hills—

you are the very best!

Thanks to all of you.

Contents

Integrity Service

Values and Ethics

- I do the right thing because it's the right thing to do.

- I put people at ease and make them feel important.

- I understand how people think and see the world.

- I view everyone as creative people who enrich my life.

- I find out what needs people have that I can help them fill.

- I take responsibility for results.

- I build and inspire those around me.

- I create extra value for customers.

- I expand my future success by tackling larger problems.

- I cause people to want to see or talk to me again.

I don't know what your destiny will be, but one thing I know: the only ones among you who will be happy are those who will have sought and found how to serve.

Dr. Albert Schweitzer

Integrity Service

Introduction

This Book Is About Your Success

We can have one of three views in all relationships:

- *It's all about* me.
- *It's all about* you.
- *It's all about* us.

The view of *me* is a self-focused one that's all about getting you to do what I want you to do for *me*. The view of *you* can be a subservient one, where I indulge you to win and myself to lose. The view of *us* is a win-win one, where I first give you the value you want and then allow you to return the value I want.

The last is the paradoxical Integrity Service view—one of mutual prosperity and abundance for everyone.

Yes, this book is about your success. It's about your life and your possibilities for enjoying more of the prosperity and abundance that await your quest.

Since you're reading this, I assume that you have a strong desire for greater success in all facets of your life—in your career, your relationships, and your personal effectiveness. I'm trusting that you're serious about your future hopes and dreams coming true.

I'll share with you time-honored principles that will surely lead you into ever-increasing levels of personal growth and goal achievement. More than 1.5 million people have participated in my personal growth courses in sixty-five nations, and what I'm offering you now is what has worked so well for them.

At this very moment, it's the level of your desire for life's richness that will determine the results you enjoy from reading these chapters.

It's not enough to simply *read* this book. The book must be *experienced*. I'll continually challenge you to spend whatever time you need on each chapter—practicing the suggestions that I'll share with you.

With a sincere desire plus application, you'll soon begin to enjoy expanded success—on and off your job.

That's my promise to you.

Why Do You Work?

Why do you do what you do? Which of the following *career views* is yours?

- *"It's spending eight hours at my job."*
- *"It's doing a good job."*
- *"It's creating value for internal and external customers."*

Each of these *career views* results from a choice you've made. This choice predetermines your job satisfaction, compensation, and success level. The *cause,* your *career choice,* is inseparable from the *effect,* your *personal degree of success.*

Every choice ultimately produces a predictable result.

Why You Succeed

Here's a success secret that many people don't *know* . . . or *practice.* They don't practice it because it runs counter to our self-focused human nature. Yet this ageless principle is unerring in its results. It always works in a paradoxical way. Here's the secret: *Your success is the by-product of the value you create for others. Your* actual *level* of success is then measured by the *amount* of benefits you create for the *most* people.

Are you disappointed with my advice? Or excited? Will you quickly dismiss it as too simplistic, or will you see it for the wisdom it contains?

If, indeed, you do understand the common sense of this eternal success principle, and if it's consistent with your values, then you're ready for this book. In the pages that follow, I'll serve as your guide and lead you through a series of thinking patterns, actions, beliefs, and behaviors that will surely elevate you to increased levels of success and personal growth . . . if you make them your own and practice them in your daily life.

Your Two Life Directions

The truth is painfully simple . . . and paradoxical. We—individuals and organizations—have two basic life directions that influence our career success and personal happiness. One is to focus on ourselves, get what we can get, and keep all we can keep. The other is to focus on others and to create as much value for them as we can, knowing that we'll be compensated, rewarded, or respected according to the amount of value we create.

Think about these two life and business views a moment. One is driven by our natural, human, ego-focus. The other evolves from an external, outer, success-oriented focus.

As you begin this book, take a few moments to review the Integrity Service Values and Ethics mentioned at the beginning of it.

After reading them, ask yourself these questions:

- *If the people in an organization practiced them, would that company be more profitable? a great place in which to work? ensured of its successful future? trusted and respected?*
- *If an individual faithfully practiced them, would he or she be more successful? more valuable to his or her organization? happier and more personally fulfilled? more highly compensated?*

If your answer to these questions is "yes," then your values are in line with the success principles of this book. You'll discover that it lays out for you a road map for your personal success with

- *external customers,*
- *internal associates,*
- *friends,*
- *family members,* and
- *relationships.*

Practicing these values-driven principles in your real-life experiences will put you into the free-flowing stream of personal and career success, happiness, and self-fulfillment. This state only comes as a result of *serendipity* — the gift of accidentally discovering good and valuable things in unexpected ways.

When you make your goal or aim to serve others, you'll discover riches that otherwise would have been hidden from you.

Success is the by-product of practicing time-proven, customer-focused behaviors that I'll share with you.

Let's begin at the beginning.

A Customer-Focused Individual

Start by defining your job as helping your organization:

1. *Get and keep satisfied, loyal customers.*
2. *Get and keep satisfied, loyal employees.*
3. *Enjoy growth and profitability.*

To the degree that you have this view of your job and make these your overall goals, you'll enjoy the elusive rewards of personal growth, high self-esteem, and increased value to your organization.

A Customer-Focused Organization

Organizations are made up of people. Organizational effectiveness results to the degree that these people can work together in a spirit of unity and harmony toward a common goal. Many organizations miss this point.

Billions of dollars are spent on organizational development. Even more billions are spent on reorganization after reorganization, driven by the assumption that once the company finds the right organizational strategy, everything will be great. So, when it isn't great, what do companies do? They call in new consultants and go through yet another reorganization.

While the proper organizational structure is important, many managers overlook a more important issue—their people. Often their people feel like mere numbers, inanimate statistical units that are passed around, handed off, and in many cases made to feel paranoid and insecure. Even in the largest of organizations, it's the development and uniting of people that get the least attention and budget, and too many organizations pay the price of this oversight.

Managers don't harness their people's energies and creativity. They can, though, by developing a customer-focused organization. This gives people a common vision that transcends their own self-focus.

Take a look at the following "Customer-Focused Organizations" model. Let me explain the model.

1. *The purpose of any organization is to serve its owners or stakeholders with growth and profitability. To do this, the organization must get and keep loyal, profitable customers and loyal, productive employees.*
2. *The point of contact includes anyone who touches customers.*
3. *The pillars of the organization are the people and systems that make up the different departments and divisions. They must view their jobs as supporting those who touch customers.*
4. *The foundation is the company's mission, vision, and core values.*

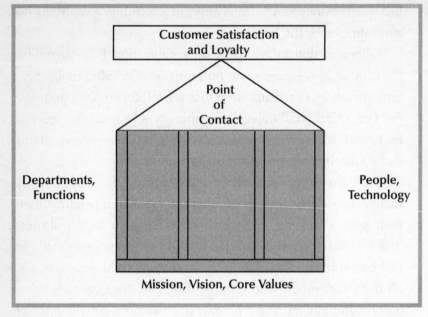

Customer-Focused Organizations

Organizations achieve their growth and profitability goals to the extent to which everyone works together, synergistically, to help get and keep loyal customers and employees.

A few years ago the *Harvard Business Review* published an article called "Putting the Service-Profit Chain to Work." The service-profit chain established the links in the chain that lead to growth and profitability. Here are the separate links:

- *Growth and profitability* are driven by
- *Customer loyalty*, which comes from
- *Customer satisfaction*, which is driven by
- *Value* provided to customers, which comes from
- *Employee productivity*, which is driven by
- *Employee loyalty*, which is caused by
- *Employee satisfaction*, which is driven by
- *Internal quality*, which is a result of
- *Leadership*.

The study points out the sequence that leads to growth and profitability. It also makes the point that a "chain is only as strong as its weakest link." This means that all the links must be healthy in order for an organization to be vital and productive.

Examine each of these links, and you'll see that it must be valued before it can be actualized into strategies or results. You'll also notice that some of the links are overlooked in the allocation of training budgets and importance to senior managers.

It's people who do all this. So here's where you come in, and where you establish your individual value. Your worth to your organization will be determined by the extent to which you know these factors:

1. *Who your customers are.*
2. *What their unique needs are.*
3. *Why they choose to do business with you.*
4. *What unique value you give them that they can't get elsewhere.*
5. *How well your role creates value for customers or supports the people who directly touch customers.*

How well you understand these five elements will determine your value to your organization, as well as the compensation or rewards you enjoy.

It is my hope that this book will help you discover the path to greater fulfillment and success—on and off your job.

By following the Action Guides that I'll share with you, you'll make larger and larger deposits into the bank account of value that you've created for others. The balance of this account, as it exceeds your withdrawals, will pay you compounded interest many times over. The wealth of value delivered to others will then serve you by causing greater self-respect, respect from others, and a reputation for integrity, responsibility, and compassion—and, along the way, increased compensation or other rewards.

What You'll Learn in This Book

You'll learn several models and communication principles. First is the G. *Val Hi* complete customer communication model. G. *Val Hi* stands for these steps:

- Greet *customers*
- Value *customers*
- Ask *how to help customers*
- Listen *to customers*
- Help *customers*
- Invite *customers back*

We'll weave this system through all the other chapters in this book.

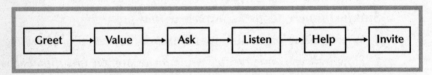

The G. *Val Hi System*

Rules for Using the System

How you use this system is important.

1. *Totally focus on the person.*
2. *Complete each step before going to the next one.*
3. *Never jump to a step without completing the previous ones.*

Sounds simple, doesn't it? Simple, maybe, but just go out and analyze ten contacts with service people and see if they do more than two or three of these steps. When you consciously complete each of these steps, you'll give people a better experience than they receive in most other places.

You'll learn a four-step problem-solving process, shown in the following "Problem-Solving Formula."

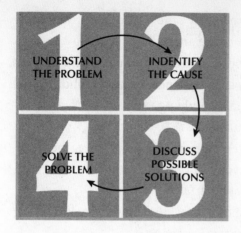

The Problem-Solving Formula

You'll find applying this simple, logical process, complete with Action Guides, will assist you in enjoying successful outcomes.

Since so much of your success involves communicating with people, you'll also learn and apply a simple behavioral style language. You'll learn how to unconsciously adapt your natural style to fit those of other people. You'll understand and communicate with them most effectively. It's all there in Chapter 3.

This book will also help you with other customer-focused and personal-growth models for you to apply in your everyday role.

But let's get to the real issue.

It Gets Down to Who You Are, Not Just What You Know

To achieve your maximum success with internal and external customers, it really gets down to *who* you are! Good customer service isn't just a strategy or even a matter of following a set of rules. There are deeper causes that drive successful behaviors.

Let's think of these three causal levels:

1. What *you know*.
2. How *you handle your emotions*.
3. What *beliefs, values, and ethical principles guide you*.

This book differs from almost any other customer service book in that it deals with all three of the above levels—not just superficial, surface ones. It'll show you how to practice effective success strategies, how to handle your emotional responses, and how to clarify and access the deeper, underlying values, beliefs, and ethical principles that drive your success.

We'll learn about the three parts of you—or, rather, the three parts that make up the one you—the *intellectual, emotional,* and *creative/unconscious,* in Chapter 1.

By practicing the suggestions in each chapter, you'll develop the strengths that will ensure your success.

What's Different About This Book?

There are enough *customer service* books published to make all the people who serve customers totally perfect—which of course they aren't!

So why does the world need another?

Most books deal with very surface-level behaviors: *Do this. Don't do that. Paint a plastic smile on your face.* That is clearly not the answer.

The problem is that as people we don't always practice what we *know.* Our actual behaviors are motivated by who we *are*— our values, beliefs, views of our own possibilities, feelings of worthiness, and other internal factors.

This book goes much deeper—into the real causes of success on and off the job. But you won't get them simply by reading. You'll grow inside this way:

Learning concepts
+ Applying them in your life
= Enjoying personal growth

It's your personal growth that will help you advance. It's more *who* you are than *what* you know.

Results Are What Count

My organization, Integrity Systems, receives feedback from all over the world about the results individuals and organizations enjoy from our unique developmental processes. Following are a few results of practicing the concepts that have been reported to us.

Employee turnover at the Tennessee Valley Region of the American Red Cross dropped from 80.4 to 26.5 percent in its Hospital Services Division. In its Blood Collection Division, employee turnover dropped from 40.9 to 22.7 percent. In the Central Plains Region of American Red Cross, employee turnover dropped from 48 to 25 percent. The Penn-Jersey Region reported the achievement of its blood collection goal for the first time in eight years, increasing collections by 8.2 percent.

Princor Financial Services, a member of the Principal Financial Group in Des Moines, Iowa, showed a 35 percent increase in overall customer effectiveness and a 32 percent increase in providing service beyond customer expectations.

Price Chopper, a supermarket chain headquartered in Schenectady, New York, reported an increase in customer service effectiveness of 21.96 percent and decreased employee turnover of 79 percent. These numbers are astounding.

Arvida, the giant home-building company based in Boca Raton, Florida, increased referral business 14.2 percent and enjoyed an increase in customer satisfaction of 25.7 percent.

The Southern Company (Georgia Power, Alabama Power, Mississippi Power) reported an increase in service level from 64.0 to 83.8 percent. Its consumer value increased from 61.6 to 65.1 percent. Georgia Power's internal service scores rose from 4.0 to 5.6 after they implemented our service program.

A chain of credit unions reported that *teller error* was reduced 40 percent.

UCLA Medical Center reported moving from the 28th percentile, compared with the other academic medical centers, to the 78th percentile, according to the Picker Patient Satisfaction Survey.

The Richardson Regional Medical Center went from being last among eleven Baylor facilities to maintaining a top ranking in patient satisfaction.

What about individual people?

Charles Wilcox, Executive Director of the Tennessee Valley Region of the American Red Cross, summed it up well: "We have already seen a difference in the teamwork between departments, better understanding between people, and greater appreciation for how each of us helps make each other's job possible."

In a manner that's typical of individuals in all organizations with whom we work, the people at Norway Savings Bank in Maine described their individual benefits like this: "More self-confidence." "Willingness to take more responsibility." "More friendly." "Happier." "Personal growth." "Goal oriented." "Improved listening skills." "More at ease with each other." "Better team players." "Better self-esteem." "More energetic." "Not placing blame." "Increased ability to cope with stress."

In addition to their reported personal benefits, we hear even more profound results: Job advancement. Mended marriages. Repaired personal relationships. Commitment to getting help with substance abuse or addiction problems that had been unaddressed.

People grow: They become more successful, enjoy life more, reach higher goals, and discover new talents and abilities.

HOW TO GAIN THE MOST FROM THIS BOOK

This book is to be *experienced*, not just *read*. To do that, please consider these suggestions.

- *Read and then review a chapter as often as necessary, maybe even several times for a week.*
- *Don't hesitate to underline, highlight, and make action notes in the margins.*
- *Assess your thoughts, feelings, and behaviors each week, using the Self-Assessment guide at the end of each chapter.*
- *Practice the Action Guides in your everyday life—both at and away from the job.*
- *Evaluate your practice at the end of each day in the Daily Success Diary pages at the end of each chapter.*
- *Go to the next chapter the next week.*
- *Don't just breeze through the book and put it aside. After reading all twelve chapters, reread those sections that you may still be a bit hazy about.*

By following these suggestions, you'll continually learn, grow, and get better. You'll find that the more you *learn,* the more you'll *learn* what there is to *learn!* Success-oriented people always discover that the room for growth expands as they move further into success.

One more thing: What you'll learn in this book can be *experientially* learned on many levels. Although the concepts are fairly simple, it's in the *application* that we discover their profound nature and that the actual benefits happen.

As you sincerely practice the principles of this book, the inviolable law of reciprocity will increasingly shower you with many benefits, guaranteeing your success in your career, your relationships, and—most important—with yourself.

You'll discover in the crucible of your life experiences an emotional understanding of an old Hindu proverb: *Those who give have all things; those who withhold have nothing.*

... if you do what is right—even if it costs you in the short run—it will pay off in the long run. (Dr. Ken Blanchard and Dr. Norman Vincent Peale, *The Power of Ethical Management*)

1 Pursue Integrity

Do the Right Thing Because It's the Right Thing to Do

I took my car into Phoenix Motors for a periodic checkup and to get the muffler repaired after a houseguest hit a wall with it while backing up and rammed the tail pipe through the muffler. When I picked the car up, the service person, Rolf Schurmer, told me that to replace the whole assembly would have cost more than $750. He explained that when he looked at it, he saw that he could have it repaired for about $35 at a welding shop.

He said it was now "good as new" and that this is what he'd have done had it been his car.

Why did he do that? Didn't it cost his company $715? Would I have paid him $750 if he had told me that was what it took to fix the car? Yes—how would I have known the difference?

Was that good for his business? Absolutely! I wouldn't take my Mercedes to any other dealer for service, nor would I buy one from another dealer. Before and after this experience, I've bought four cars from the folks at Phoenix Motors and have had all my service work done by them. I wouldn't trust my work to anyone except Rolf and Gordon Payne. Their honesty and my trust that they'll treat me as they'd want to be treated have made their company lots of money from me.

Just as for them, your success with customers, or anyone else's, is heightened as your choices, decisions, and actions are driven by sound, customer-focused values—most important, those of integrity.

What Is Integrity?

As this chapter's title says, *integrity* is simply doing the right thing because it's the right thing to do. To have integrity is to align your thoughts and choices with strong values to create right behaviors. To integrate your *inner* with your *outer*. To make your outer behaviors congruent with your inner values and guiding life principles.

This chapter deals with doing the right thing for people—customers, associates, or others with whom we associate. We'll look at several attitudes, motives, values, or ethics as ways to practice *integrity*.

Sound too simple considering today's rough-and-tumble, dog-eat-dog world? Then look around you at corporate scandals and personal lies that come back to multiply problems for people who attempted to cover up the truth.

Think about these questions:

- *What did a lie cost President Richard Nixon?*
- *What did a lie cost President Bill Clinton?*
- *What did "cooked books" cost Enron, Global Crossing, and WorldCom?*
- *What did shading the truth about selling more than $200,000 in stocks cost Martha Stewart?*

- *What deceptive practices brought down the venerable Arthur Andersen firm?*
- *How many tens of millions of dollars did it cost insurance companies because their agents misled customers?*
- *Why did it cost Sears Auto Centers an estimated $60 million for failure to clarify the line between legitimate preventive maintenance and unnecessary service?*

And on, and on, and on.

Look at the devastation created by a few corporate executives, and how it wreaked financial havoc on thousands of innocent people. Think about the billions lost in corporate value and the life savings of hard-working people that were wiped out. Examine the arrogance of a few executives who made decisions to loan themselves hundreds of millions of dollars for large yachts, French Impressionist paintings, palatial estates, and who knows what else.

Then . . . answer the question: *Is lack of integrity bad for business?*

Is Lack of Integrity Bad for Business?

Turning from corporate scandals, let's look at real life. What about the student who cheats on an exam? The small-business person who lies about his profits on his income tax return? The husband who cheats on his wife? The pusher who gets junior high kids started on drugs? The teenager working at McDonald's who occasionally slips a five-dollar bill in his pocket?

Or consider the Major League player who illegally abuses his body with steroids, the batter who "corks" his bat, the world-class track star who takes illegal substances, or the athlete who gets caught in a gambling habit and shaves points in a game.

Or how about the author who has other people write a book

and puts his or her own name on it, pretending it is entirely his own work? Or the person who lies to himself, saying "I don't have a problem . . . I can quit any time I want to" or "Taking tools from the auto dealership where I work is okay; the boss makes more money now than he knows what to do with"?

Do we have a problem here? Do these behaviors contribute to the betterment, enlightenment, or success of people? How cheated are the recipients of such behaviors? What effect do they have on the people who make these choices? How do they create a diminishment of the values of our entire culture?

Is lack of integrity bad for a successful life? When moral and ethical principles are violated, is there a destructive fallout? Does this prevent people from being all they were meant to be? What are the effects when basic spiritual laws are violated? Laws of equity? Laws of life?

Can people really cheat others and not cheat themselves even more? Is there a cause and effect? "The thief steals from himself," wrote Emerson. "The swindler swindles himself." Can we do wrong without suffering wrong?

After thinking about the question "Is lack of integrity bad for business and life?" maybe the answer to the question "Is integrity good for business and life?" becomes clearer.

Values-Driven Behaviors: Doing the Right Thing for Others

Benjamin Franklin once wrote "Well done is better than well said." The same is true of values and ethical behaviors—doing them beats talking about them.

In the large scheme of things, success principles are carefully hidden in simple, ethical actions, attitudes, and behaviors. They lie silently and obscurely awaiting discovery and practice before they can release their power. True success quietly sits on the park bench of life, revealing its secret powers only to those who diligently seek it through service.

It is only by valuing service to others that we discover a truth: *We enrich ourselves the most when we serve others.* This is a paradox that only those who seek wisdom discern.

Our discovery of this truth brings with it the obligation to do the right thing in all situations. I learned this from W. Clement Stone, a very wise, successful man.

In 1980 I was privileged to go to Chicago for six months as a consultant for Mr. Stone's company. The great book he wrote with Napoleon Hill, entitled *Success through a Positive Mental Attitude*, had helped me completely change my life about fifteen years earlier.

Mr. Stone strictly adhered to a set of values in his personal and business life. Sitting in on many of his meetings and conferences where problems or questions came up, I heard him ask, "What is the right thing to do?" The discussion would then center around his question. Once all agreed on the right thing to do, he would announce in his high-pitched, authoritative voice, "Then we will do the right thing, because it's the right thing to do."

At this point, the discussion about what to do would be over, and the group would move on to taking action and *doing the right thing*.

Let's explore some of these serendipitous, self-enriching behaviors, attitudes, and actions: dealing fairly with others, dealing honestly with others, and knowing your internal and external customers.

Dealing Fairly with Others

One of the great lessons I've learned in customer service was taught to me many years ago by a very wise gentleman whose name was Claude Hooks. Mr. Hooks, as I called him, because it fit the respect I had for him, mowed and maintained my lawn each week. Mr. Hooks had great integrity. With little or no education, he had put all seven of his children through college by doing lawn maintenance.

Each Friday evening, when he had all his equipment loaded in his truck, he'd knock on my door, tell me he had finished, and ask me to look at everything to make sure I was satisfied. Of course, I was always satisfied and would tell him so. Then I'd ask him, "Mr. Hooks, how much do I owe you?"

He'd look into my eyes and kindly reply, "Oh, Mr. Willingham, just whatever you think it's worth." He'd pause a moment and then say, "I know you'll be fair."

Oh, man, how could I handle that? I'm sure I paid him twice what other people would have charged. How could I live with myself if I hadn't done that?

Obviously, Mr. Hooks believed in *fair dealing*. He dealt fairly with me and gave me the opportunity to reciprocate. How could I have ever violated his expectations of fairness from me? If I had, I'd have been looking for another person to do my work.

I'm sure there were people who would have tried to take advantage of him, but they wouldn't fit the profile of who he'd accept as a customer.

Dealing Honestly with Others

Not long ago I got a call from a man whom I had not seen for over ten years. We chatted for a couple of moments, and then he said, "Listen, there's something that I've felt guilty about and have wanted to talk to you about for several years.

"Remember when you made the proposal for a customer service program for us?"

"Yes, I do."

"Well, you'll remember that my boss at the time spent $300,000 on a research project to prove that higher customer satisfaction would be good for profitability. He wanted to have the results to back up his going ahead with the program."

"Yes, I remember," I replied.

"When we got the study back, it said nothing. It was poorly designed and was obviously done by people who didn't know what they were doing."

"Okay," I said, beginning to get the drift of his call.

"Well, when he saw that he'd spent the money on a poor project, he buried it in a file and scratched your project. If he had continued with your program, he would have had to show people the study, and that would have revealed that he had wasted the money. That's why he abruptly cut you off. I knew about it, had to keep my mouth shut, and have felt guilty ever since. I'm now in a new job, and my telling you the truth can't have any repercussions for me. And . . . it now gets all this off my chest."

How would you like to have someone waste $300,000 of your money to cover his own rear?

All of us have moments where we're tempted to shade the truth a bit—usually to avoid sharing "bad news" with others. There's something about the nature of ego-focused humanity that doesn't want others to find out any "bad news" of our own creation.

I once had people in my own organization falsify sales to make themselves look good, receive bonuses, or reach sales and profit goals they'd committed to hitting. Financially, their dishonesty cost me many times more than it profited them.

But in the end, all my business partner and I lost was a couple of million dollars. They lost people's trust and respect, and I'm guessing they also lost some self-respect.

BE ABOVEBOARD ON ALL ACTIONS

In cases like those I've just mentioned, if the people had simply come to me and my partner and said, "We have a problem.
Here it is. We want your understanding and help in solving it,"
things would have been different. But they didn't. No apologies.
No remorse. No attempt to make things right. Instead, they attempted to cover things up, which, of course, only prolonged and
compounded the problem.

As I've watched people try to cover up their indiscretions, blun-
ders, or overt mistakes, I'm often reminded of Emerson's great
words in his essay "Compensation."

> Commit a crime, and the earth is made of glass. Commit a
> crime, and it seems as if a coat of snow fell on the ground, such
> as reveals in the woods the track of every partridge and fox and
> squirrel and mole.

He also wrote, "You cannot do wrong without suffering
wrong."

Really? In real life? With man-eating sharks in the waters that
we daily swim in?

LIVE SO OTHERS BELIEVE YOU ARE HONORABLE
AND ABOVEBOARD

As I speak before groups about trust and respect, I often ask
rhetorically, "What do we do to earn people's trust and respect?"
My answer is "By being the kind of people that others *can* trust
and respect."

You see, it's not *what* we say; rather, it's *who* we are.

I've worked with many honorable, upright people. Unfortunately, I've also worked with some who weren't honorable and
upright. My experience is that those who talk most about their
piety, honesty, or integrity are the ones you should probably

watch. I've worked with men who could eloquently romance the virtues of integrity, only to later discover that their real-life behaviors didn't match their advice to others. Maybe they couldn't keep their eyes and hands off the little "ewe lambs" they were "shepherding." Or they couldn't control their habits, appetites, or thirsts.

While none of us is perfect, the people I respect the most are those who attempt to live their values, rather than talk about them.

For years, I had a wonderful business partner in Bernard Petty. In more than twenty years of partnership we never had a single argument, conflict, or disagreement. He handled all our money. I trusted him completely, because he was completely trustworthy. I absolutely knew that should he err, it would be in my favor.

Bernard never ducked sticky issues with our sales and marketing people. His integrity, honesty, and sense of right always kept him from getting into adversarial relationships. All our people respected him so much that they wouldn't allow communications to dip into anger or finger pointing.

His high self-esteem kept him from putting others down or getting into conflicts with them. His actions and responses were always honorable and aboveboard, because he was an honorable, aboveboard person.

Bernard Petty's actions spoke for themselves. He had no need to broadcast them. He was a lucky man—having a wife and support person in Laverne, who also shares his values.

LET YOUR ATTITUDES AND ACTIONS SPEAK FOR THEMSELVES

A number of years ago, while riding with a friend in his new car, I asked him why he chose this particular model. He explained that he actually preferred a different brand, but he wanted to do business with Ernie Winton. I was looking for a new car and didn't know Ernie Winton, but I thought, He sounds like someone you can trust. So I went to see him.

Ernie took his time helping me select a new model and told me about some of his long-term customers. I bought with very little price discussion.

For the two or so years that I owned that car, when it was time for service, Ernie would call me and say, "It's time for a service; if it's okay, I'll pick up your car, leave my demonstrator, and return your car after we're finished with it."

Can you believe that? I'd never had another car salesperson do that for me. Is it any mystery that he had a long list of satisfied customers?

What can you do, after your customers have bought from you, to silently demonstrate your extra-mile philosophy?

Several years ago I designed a customer trade-replacement process for Chevrolet. Typically, when people bought a car and had problems that the dealer couldn't or didn't fix, they'd call an 800 number and register their complaint. Occasionally, the dealer wouldn't satisfy the customer, and the case would go to arbitration, with people pitted against each other. Nobody ended up feeling good. It cost Chevrolet around $18,000 then just to settle a claim in this process. Customers were often left angry, vowing never to buy another Chevrolet.

We designed a process in which a Chevrolet Zone person would call customers, listen intently, understand their situations, let them vent, and genuinely attempt to work out a win-win situation. The Zone person would call the selling dealer and work out a deal where the dealer took the car back and gave the customer a new one. The dealer would agree to repair and sell the used car for no profit, and Chevrolet would reimburse the dealer for any actual loss in the transaction. Customers were asked to pay only for the miles on the car that they'd driven.

This process cost Chevrolet an average of only $1,700 instead of $18,000, and most important, the company kept loyal customers. It also allowed Chevrolet and its dealers to back up their promise of service excellence. Here was another way to actually deliver customer satisfaction, not just talk about it.

Never Use "Truth" to Hurt Another Person

I once knew a person who was very negative, cynical, and perfectionistic. This person could spot flaws in other people with great finesse. What he prided himself on—his ability to see through people's hidden, devious meanings—he used as an excuse to find fault with them. He justified all this with the explanation that he believed in telling the truth.

Unfortunately, his "truth" was in reality meant to hurt people. I suppose focusing on other people's inadequacies was his way of hiding his own flaws. When some truth is used to hurt another person, it can be very destructive—actually, more to the sender than to the recipient.

Do you know people who are quick to point out your flaws? I'll bet you do. Don't you just crave being around them?

We see politicians doing this so often that maybe we think that it's the way for us to "gain votes." The problem is that people to whom we direct this supposed truth about themselves are usually hurt rather than helped. Add to that the fact that when people "reveal the truth" to us about another person, we wonder what they're "revealing" to others about us.

A good rule of thumb is this: *If telling the truth hurts another person, don't tell it.*

Straight Talk with Integrity

My good friend Barry Griswell, chairman, CEO, and president of Principal Financial Group in Des Moines, Iowa, instituted a policy he refers to as "Straight Talk," based on his belief that honest, open communication is often lost in the business world.

Straight Talk is

- *Clearly expressing your viewpoint.*
- *Establishing an atmosphere where employees can freely ask questions and present opinions that may be unpopular.*
- *Encouraging people to build on other employees' ideas by generating healthy discussion.*

Straight Talk isn't

- *About saying everything to everyone at any time, regardless of the consequences.*
- *About power.*
- *A license to be antagonistic.*
- *Ruthless or demanding.*

Barry Griswell emphasizes, "It is vital that we have an environment where feedback can freely flow in order to help all of us fulfill our potential."

All employees learn these seven principles of *Straight Talk*:

1. Take personal responsibility. *When you know something is going wrong and there is a better way—say so! Talk to the people who can change things—not everyone else who can't. Have the courage to speak up if that will make a difference.*

2. Manage your emotions. *Keep your emotions out of it. Straight talk isn't about you (or them). It's about building a better business relationship or finding a better solution.*

3. Be tactful. *Straight Talk is about effectively conveying information and ideas. Think about others' feelings, but don't let that stifle your use of Straight Talk.*

4. Avoid spin. *Don't use only the information that backs up your point of view. Give the whole story—good and bad—then clearly state how you've reached your conclusions.*

5. Stick to the facts. *Straight Talk isn't about personalities. Focus on the issue, not the people involved.*

6. Make Straight Talk a habit. *It's easier to use Straight Talk ef-*

fectively if you do it often. You become more alert to situations that need Straight Talk.

7. Listen. *Remember that you're not the only one entitled to use Straight Talk. You have a responsibility to listen to others, as well. Straight Talk is about exchanging ideas to form the best solutions.*

The results of this have been extremely positive and helpful in interpersonal communication at the Principal Financial Group.

Where Do Your Values Reside?

Our values reveal who we are. They reside in the deepest parts of us. They silently motivate most of our actions and choices.

In the introduction I suggested that there are three parts of us: the *intellectual, emotional,* and *creative/unconscious.* Let's call these the "I Think," the "I Feel," and the "I Am," as in "The Three Dimensions of Human Behavior" model that follows.

With your "I Think," you make decisions, exercise logic, and learn information. With your "I Feel" you exhibit emotions, feelings, and moods. Your "I Am" houses your unconscious self-image—your internal beliefs about

- *who you are,*
- *what it's possible for you to achieve,* and
- *what you deserve to enjoy in terms of life rewards.*

Your values—your beliefs about what's right and wrong—are in your "I Am." Your emotional controls, your physical and spiritual thermostat, your emotional and spiritual DNA are all in this unconscious *set point* within you.

The programming in your "I Am" dimension controls all your actions, feelings, behavior, and abilities. This incredibly powerful part within you determines your actual level of success more than your knowledge, experience, and education do.

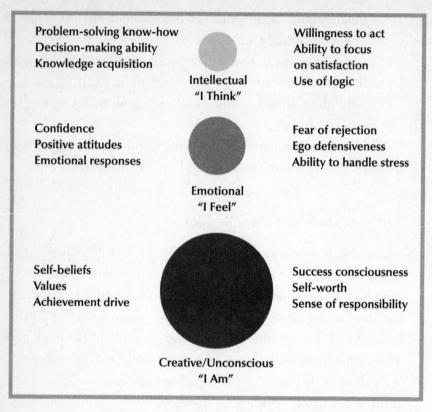

Problem-solving know-how
Decision-making ability
Knowledge acquisition

Intellectual
"I Think"

Willingness to act
Ability to focus
on satisfaction
Use of logic

Confidence
Positive attitudes
Emotional responses

Emotional
"I Feel"

Fear of rejection
Ego defensiveness
Ability to handle stress

Self-beliefs
Values
Achievement drive

Creative/Unconscious
"I Am"

Success consciousness
Self-worth
Sense of responsibility

The Three Dimensions of Human Behavior

This internal driver of your external success isn't changed or developed by *intellectual knowledge*. It's been programmed *experientially* and is only changed by structuring certain new experiences in your everyday life. Understand this and you'll quickly see why this book is an *action* one. It isn't designed to teach as much as it is to lead you through successful experiences.

Integrity as a Success Strategy

The few organizations or people who resort to unethical or deceptive business practices often draw the public's attention away from the thousands of other companies and individuals who succeed by constantly giving honest value to their customers.

Many people and politicians throw stones at pharmaceutical companies for price gouging. We don't often hear of examples such as Merck, which a few years ago did something very different. Merck scientists discovered a drug that would cure a parasite that causes a disease called *river blindness*. The victims of this disease develop severe pain, eventually leading to blindness.

Soon the company found out that the people who needed this drug couldn't afford it. At a cost of millions, Merck decided to give the drug away to people who needed it.

Merck's response was this: "We try never to forget that medicine is for people. It is not for profits. The profits follow, and if we remember that, they have never failed to appear. The better we have remembered it, the larger they have been."

This great company's statement underscores a key principle of free enterprise: *Focus on giving value to customers while managing your business sensibly, and profits are the result. The more value you give, the more profit you should enjoy.*

The Key to Your Success

How do you differentiate yourself in the service you give to your internal associates and external customers? How valuable is your touch with external customers or internal associates? Exactly whom do you support or serve? What are their names? What do they want or need that you can give them? How can you give them extra value?

Your success depends on how you answer the preceding questions with your attitudes, motives, and actions.

When I was in college, an accounting professor, Dr. Overton Faubus, taught me much more about success in *life* than he did about *accounting*. I still don't know the difference between a debit and a credit, but I learned one lesson from him that has served me infinitely. With a business background, rather than an academic one, he told us several times that whatever we do, we should seek to go the extra mile in all our actions. In his wisdom he knew this was a powerful success factor. At the time I wasn't mature enough to totally understand the depth of power contained in his advice, but I did look for ways to follow it.

I worked afternoons at an office supply and printing company, earning 65 cents an hour. I loved the job because it gave me a chance to meet customers. The hours flew by each day.

Fresh from Dr. Faubus's advice one day, I walked in the side door of the Pender Company, which led through the heating and air-conditioning equipment room. From there, a door went into the company's storeroom. A big pile of dirt and trash had blown into the equipment room—the "boiler room," as we called it. Everyone had been walking by it, without noticing it or doing anything about it, for weeks. It was a mess.

Noticing the trash and dirt, and remembering that I didn't have classes the next day, I decided to come in and clean it up. The next morning I showed up in old jeans, and as I walked into the store Mr. Pender looked at me and asked gruffly, "What are you doing coming in here looking like that? You're not supposed to be here until twelve-thirty!"

"I don't have classes this morning, sir, so I thought I'd come in and clean out the boiler room," I said as I walked by him.

I got a push broom, a dustpan, and a trash barrel and went to work. It was dusty and nasty. I was sneezing, wheezing, and coughing. In a bit, Mr. Pender came back and looked at me. "What are you doing?" he asked.

"Cleaning out the boiler room," I replied.

"Who told you to do this?" he asked.

"No one."

"Then why are you doing it?"

"Because it's dirty and needs cleaning."

He shook his head, his questions still not answered, shifted his ever-present cigar, made some noise clearing his throat, and walked away.

The next Friday he personally handed me my paycheck, displaying as close to a smile as I ever saw on his face, and said, "You'll notice something different in this check."

I opened the check and saw that I had received a 10-cent-an-hour raise.

I'm not sure I learned anything else in college that approached that lesson.

Who was my customer? Who did I need to please? Did going the extra mile pay off for me? Did it cause me to be more valuable? Did it build my self-esteem?

Knowing Who Your Customers Are

The first step for an organization to be customer-focused is for all employees to know who their customers are. This may sound simple, but ask ten people who their organization's customers are and you'll get blank stares from about two-thirds of them. Rarely will they tell you about internal people whom they serve.

The truth is that most people just see their jobs as functions they do. They don't see the reason *why* they do them. When people can look past their jobs and see that their purpose is either to satisfy customers or to support those who directly touch customers, a transformation occurs. They feel a greater sense of meaning, fulfillment, and value.

Paradoxically, the human spirit is nourished by serving and

creating value for others much more than by taking it for ourselves. Rewards, appreciation, and pay are all more meaningful when we receive them for extra services rendered than if we just get them for doing a job.

Millions of workers are robbed of joy and job satisfaction because they just go to work, do whatever they have to do to get by, with no heart or purpose in it, and then leave as soon as quitting time occurs. This myopic, misguided attitude often says "Pay me more for less work" and robs people of any sense of fulfillment, job satisfaction, or reason for advancement.

Southwest Airlines people are trained well to never forget who their external customers are, and they do many innovative activities to make unique touch points. With increased security screening at airports, along with increased technology, Southwest Airlines implemented kiosks where customers can punch in information and get boarding passes. These have passengers' names, and their boarding order. I noticed that when I presented my driver's license, along with my boarding pass, the boarding agents would look at both, tear off my ticket stub, hand both back, look into my eyes, and say, "Thank you for flying with us today, Ron."

All of a sudden I felt special.

They also know who their *internal* customers are. I've carefully watched how their ticket agents, flight attendants, and pilots interact with each other. They announce each other's birthdays, team up to sing songs, and have fun together.

Herb Kelleher knew and preached: "You can't have excellent customer satisfaction without great employee satisfaction." Their profitability is a tribute to his belief.

As you read through the following ways to expand your value to your customers and your organization, please consider what I believe to be a law of compensation: *The more you can know who your customers are and what their needs are, and then focus on cre-*

ating extra value for them, the more you'll raise your value to your organization.

As you do this, in the law of life, you'll enjoy many forms of greater compensation.

LEARN THEIR NEEDS, WANTS, PROBLEMS, OR GOALS

The next step on the success-with-customers ladder is to identify their unique needs. This is another way of saying that you learn from each customer how he wants to be treated.

For several years I took my shirts and dry cleaning to a place that was on my way to work. It was convenient to drop them off, but I was never really happy with the way they came back. If I asked for medium starch, they came back stiff as a board. If I ordered them light, they were so limp that they didn't look professionally done.

Add to that the fact that the attendant never remembered my name or did anything to make me feel as if she noticed me as a person. Never a "Hello" or a "Thank you." I'm going to guess that I was close to being a $1,000-per-year customer.

One day I asked myself, "Why am I doing this? Why don't I find another place?"

So I did. I began taking my clothes to a substation in my office building. Ampi, the attendant, was nice and friendly, and she noticed me as a human being. The third time I patronized the place, she remembered my name and how I wanted my shirts done. She also understood my need for a compromise between too stiff and too limp. The difference in treatment was amazing. I felt that my need to be noticed as an actual human being was important to her. One of my staff gave her this page of my original manuscript, and she has it framed and displayed on her counter. Now I really get special treatment.

DEVELOP A CLEAR PICTURE OF HOW YOUR JOB DIRECTLY OR INDIRECTLY AFFECTS CUSTOMER SATISFACTION OR LOYALTY

Remember the principle "The more value you create for internal or external customers, the more valuable you are to them and to your organization." The more valuable you are to your organization, the more you will provide the organization with the wherewithal to compensate you more.

To make this point let's emphasize that customers have different levels of needs. In *First, Break All the Rules*, the authors, Marcus Buckingham and Curt Coffman, mention the following hierarchy of customers' needs. According to Gallup surveys of a billion customers, over a twenty-year period, customers experience these needs:

Level 1—*At the lowest level, customers expect* accuracy.

Level 2—*The next level is* availability.

Level 3—*At this level customers expect* partnership.

Level 4—*The most advanced level of customer expectation is* advice.

Buckingham and Coffman go on to point out that if you can consistently meet the expectations of *partnership* and *advice*, you'll have transformed *prospects* into *advocates*.

If you want to be more important to your organization through service to either internal associates or external customers, first do this:

1. *Clearly identify where you are now in the size or level of needs you fill.*
2. *Relate the level of service you give with your value to your organization—in actual compensation, job security, or other benefits.*
3. *Remind yourself that if you want to increase your compensation, job security, or other benefits, you must move up the*

chain of importance by satisfying higher internal or external customer needs.

4. Develop a plan for doing this and carry it out.

The following ideas, through the end of this chapter, will help you accomplish these four steps.

Set a Goal for the Success Level You Want to Enjoy

As you begin this journey toward greater career and personal success, set clear goals for what you want to happen in your future. These are specific statements: *Who* you want to become. *What* you want to achieve. *Where* you want to go. *When* you want to achieve your goals. *What* rewards will you enjoy when you achieve them. *How* you'll go about getting where you want to go.

Take some time during this week to set some fairly short-term goals that define objective points in your future. Short-term (one- to six-month) goals are more realistic and attainable. Their gratification is more imminent. They give you more energy, commitment, enthusiasm, and drive than do longer-term goals.

Take some time to visit with a friend, an associate, your manager, or your spouse to get feedback as to what level of goals that person sees you reaching. Make sure to choose a positive person who will look at you honestly with the purpose of helping you discover greater capabilities and possibilities. Stay away from negative people or anyone who might be jealous of your successes.

Next, sit down and write some goals that cover these areas of your life:

- *Job or career*
- *Personal growth*
- *Finances*
- *Family*
- *Fun or recreation*

- *Spiritual*
- *Other*

When you set these goals, write them down like this:

- "By July 1, I will develop the skill of _____."
- "By January 1, I will save $_____ each month."
- "By April 15, I will increase my sales or productivity by _____ percent."
- "Beginning September 1, I will exercise _____ times each week."
- "By November 15, I will weigh _____ pounds."

Get the idea? State your goals in positive statements. Be sure to include what you'll achieve, become, or do by a certain date. These then become self-suggestions you can repeat over and over to yourself, thus programming them deep within your unconscious.

This activity carries out a principle that you'll hear more about in this book: *What we feed our minds, we become!*

HOW TO GAIN THE MOST FROM THIS CHAPTER

The life principles we've discussed are timeless and contain universal truths that aren't commonly known, discovered, or valued by less discerning people. They may even sound elementary and powerless when only considered conceptually. But when practiced, they vitalize your feelings and emotions. In short, to comprehend their value, they must be *experienced*, not just *intellectually learned*.

Review this chapter, highlighting items and making notes about how you can practice its concepts. You might make some notes on cards or on your computer as a reminder to practice them. Do the Self-Assessment that follows here. Then score yourself on the Daily Success Diary at the end of this chapter each day.

This is a simple yet powerful developmental process. You'll discover that following these steps will help you move past just *knowing* these values to *developing habits* that will become part of your automatic thinking and response patterns. Day by day you'll grow, learn, and become more important to your organization.

Remember, it isn't what you *know*, it's who you *are* that drives your success, and this is silently communicated to your external customers and your internal associates.

Self-Assessment: *Pursue Integrity* ✐ ✎

Take a moment to read each of the following statements. Then circle the number that best describes your actions or thoughts, with *1* being "Never" and *10* being "Always."

1. I attempt to do the right thing in all situations.

   1   2   3   4   5   6   7   8   9   10

2. I have a strong set of personal values and ethics.

   1   2   3   4   5   6   7   8   9   10

3. I believe that honesty is the best policy.

   1   2   3   4   5   6   7   8   9   10

4. I believe that all my actions bring their own rewards.

   1   2   3   4   5   6   7   8   9   10

5. I attempt to *live* my values and not *talk* about them.

   1   2   3   4   5   6   7   8   9   10

6. I never use "truth" to hurt another person.

   1   2   3   4   5   6   7   8   9   10

7. I attempt to go the extra mile in all transactions.

   1   2   3   4   5   6   7   8   9   10

8. I compliment the behaviors of associates who act with integrity.

   1   2   3   4   5   6   7   8   9   10

9. I see my job as creating internal and external customer loyalty.

   1   2   3   4   5   6   7   8   9   10

10. I set goals for specific ways I can create value for others.

   1   2   3   4   5   6   7   8   9   10

Action Guide: *Daily Success Diary*

Pursue Integrity

Please score yourself from 1 to 10 for each daily action, with
1 being "Never" and *10* being "Always."

	S	M	T	W	T	F	S
1. Dealing fairly with others:							
a. I listened to others' opinions and feelings.							
b. I saw the world through their eyes and ears.							
c. I did the right thing because it's the right thing to do.							
2. Dealing honestly with others:							
a. I was aboveboard in all actions.							
b. I attempted to live so others believe I am honorable and aboveboard.							
c. I let my upright actions speak for themselves.							
3. Knowing your customers:							
a. I know who my internal and external customers are.							

(continued on next page)

	S	M	T	W	T	F	S
3. Knowing your customers: *(continued)*							
b. I learned what their needs, wants, problems, or goals are.							
c. I went the extra mile in all situations.							
Total each day							

The time men spend trying to impress others they could spend in doing the things by which others would be impressed. (Frank Romey)

2 Greet Customers

Put People at Ease and Make
Them Feel Important

One of my favorite restaurants in New York City is Giambelli's, a block east of Saks Fifth Avenue. Mr. Frank Giambelli, the owner, must be in his eighties as I'm writing this. Each time I've gone in he's been there to greet me with a genuine smile and a handshake. He's gracious and charming, and he makes me feel that my choice in dining there is the best one I could have made.

Not only are his guests greeted as special people, but the ambiance of his restaurant appeals to the senses and invites customers to expect a great experience. The plethora of fresh flowers and the smells of great Italian cooking, along with the look of a unique, traditional New York restaurant, all give a first impression that dining is going to be a special treat. And it always is.

My experience with Giambelli's illustrates the importance of the first step in the G. *Val Hi* System described in the Introduction: *Greet customers.*

First Impressions

How important are first impressions? How lasting are they? Why do we often forget ten good buying experiences and remember only one bad one?

Believe it or not, while I was writing this chapter, a person came to my home to talk to me about refinishing my cabinetry and countertops. I had had an appointment with her for Friday at 5:00 P.M., which she didn't keep, but she later called and rescheduled for Saturday at 11:00 A.M.

She came in and introduced herself as the owner of the company, and the next thing she said was "If we can agree on price, are you prepared to buy today?"

I couldn't believe it. I thought that moss-covered line had long ago been dropped from used-car salesmen's sensitive, caring approaches.

"Aren't we getting ahead of things?" I asked her, only to receive a very hard-eyed stare. Her face and eyes gave off the degree of empathy and warmth that you'd get from a day-old biscuit. Her eyes were permanently fixed in one single mode—humorless.

"Maybe you'd better look at my cabinets and find out what I want," I responded, still a bit unsure whether or not she was using dry humor.

She immediately told me that she'd recommend black granite tops. I kid you not. She actually said this without even asking me what I wanted. I replied that I wouldn't want black, because it showed water spots.

Then she asked me again, "If we can come to terms on price . . ."

I still couldn't believe it. "Surely she's read one of my books and is just putting me on," I thought.

I suggested that maybe she should listen and try to understand what I wanted. This got me the response "I'm also an interior designer; I usually know what's best for people."

And then she asked her question a third time, "If we can come to terms on price, are you prepared to buy today?" She obviously did not want to waste her time if I wasn't ready to buy.

"Whoa," I responded. "I do not react well to pressure. If, once you understand what I really want, you give me a price that compares well with another company's, then, after I talk to two of your satisfied customers, I might buy. If you understand this and will quit pressuring me, I'll allow you to quote a price to me."

She then agreed to send one of her "architects" by the following Monday to give me an estimate. We agreed on a 5:00 P.M. appointment, and she asked, "Can I count on you to keep this appointment?"

It was so blatant I laughed out loud as I responded, "If you'll recall, I was here at five yesterday, and you weren't."

That sailed right past her stare.

I followed her out to get a wood sample. Her dog was in her car and began to bark like crazy at me. I got the feeling that if it could have escaped through the crack in her car window, it would have shredded me. To explain her dog's behavior, she said, "He doesn't like people."

I asked myself, "Now, who could he have picked that up from?"

This happened exactly as I've shared it. I can't make stuff like this up.

She left. I wondered if her "architect" would show up on Monday.

He did, and he was a very nice person. I eventually bought from him with one condition—that I wouldn't have to deal with the owner. It took a lot of his apologizing to move me to a decision.

Does this sound like any experience you've ever had?

How Important Are First Impressions?

Whenever I think of *first impressions*, my mind jumps back many years ago to when I owned a retail furniture and design business.

One day a wholesale manufacturer's representative came into my store and introduced himself, and the encounter has been ingrained in my mind ever since.

"Ron," he said, "my name is Jack Lopez Klein. My name is very important to me, and I'd like for you to remember it!"

His mannerisms immediately attracted my attention. He was quiet but seemed very confident. He looked directly into my eyes as he spoke. I was impressed by his sincerity.

"You can remember my name," he went on, "if you'll remember these things."

He looked at me—I had a feeling that he was checking me out to make sure I was listening.

" 'Jack' is American, and I'm proud to be an American. 'Lopez' is Spanish, and I was born in Mexico. 'Klein' is Jewish, and I'm Jewish."

Wow! How could I ever forget an introduction like that?

We sat down and continued visiting. He was much shorter than I was, and wore cowboy boots. His hair was thin to balding, his nose seemed to zigzag all over his face, and he had a malformed upper lip. Clark Gable he wasn't, but a super, genuine, professional salesperson he was.

After we chatted for a few minutes, he told me, "I see by looking around your store that my lines wouldn't fit in with the styles you carry.

"Really," he went on, "I knew that anyway, but I just wanted to come in and meet you."

He visited for a while, had some nice things to say about my store, and, in a short time, was gone. I've never seen him since.

Not long after that I noticed in a trade journal that he'd been voted the most outstanding wholesale-furniture salesman in the Southwest. I wasn't surprised.

I've thought about Jack Lopez Klein many times since then, remembering the impact his approach had on me. I can still vividly recall sitting and talking to him, wanting to buy something from him, because his manner impressed me so much.

How quickly do *you* form first impressions after you meet someone, either in person or over the telephone? How lasting are those impressions? How do they alter your own feelings or opinions about the person?

What factors influence your impressions of people? Their dress, grooming, manner, tone of voice, perceived interest in you? What else? When you think of it, many different elements contribute to your perceptions about others.

We form impressions both consciously and unconsciously— from quick observations to deeper, instinctive feelings. We often subliminally decide whether we like people, feel good about them, trust them, or want to do business with them in the first few seconds of contact.

Well, guess what? Others react to us the same way.

Let's think of some specific ways you can make the very best first impression on people—remembering that every contact or repeat encounter gives you a chance to start your communication off on the best footing.

It all begins with your intent—your values.

Value the Value of Valuing People

Want to make a positive first impression? Here's the beginning. You must *want* to create great first impressions. You must *value* the act. An important question is this: *Do you value the value of valuing people?*

That's what it takes—*valuing the value of valuing people*. It gets down to the basic, fundamental value that drives your behaviors—it's *who you are* that gives power to *what you do*. "Who you are," wrote Emerson, "speaks so loudly that I can't hear what you say."

Your character speaks *silently, yet powerfully*. You often speak louder with your character and values than with your tongue.

We all have experienced people who say the right things and have all the right moves but come across as a bit slick or hollow. You sense it when a person's greeting is genuine and heart-driven. Something deep inside you flips a switch on your intuition mechanism, and you feel that this person is special. It usually doesn't take long to feel this; it can happen in seconds.

When you communicate with people, what really gets through their filters, mental cut-off valves, and unconscious screens? How much communication takes place consciously, and how much is unconscious?

Here are some key questions you can ask yourself that can affect the first impressions you make on people:

1. *Do I see my job or role as one of helping others solve problems, fill needs, or reach goals?*
2. *Do I find personal fulfillment in this role?*
3. *Does this service role fit who I am?*
4. *Can I subordinate all my other responsibilities, duties, or work processes to that of understanding people's needs and helping to fill them?*
5. *Do I value putting people above processes?*
6. *Do I view each contact as a way to enjoy a unique person?*

Answering the preceding questions can reveal your values. Your answers will also influence deep levels within you, which will then drive your actual behaviors. You alone will make decisions as to how you answer these questions in your real-life interactions with people.

As you think about how values drive your outer behaviors, let's think about some basic, simple, everyday actions that, when done with a sincere desire to help people, will insure your successful communication with others.

Make Eye Contact

It has often been said that the eyes are the mirrors of the soul, revealing the unique essence of a person. They connect you with people's hearts, feelings, and thoughts. On a less complex level, they give you a target on which to focus your attention, a specific place to put your own eyes.

It's difficult to look into people's eyes, desiring to connect with them, and think of anything other than them. Looking people in the eye not only honors them; it also allows you to tune into them. Eye contact helps you lay the foundation for a great first impression.

Okay, I know what some of you are thinking—"I don't see my customers face to face."

I understand. Roughly 40 percent of all the participants in our sales and customer service programs have only telephone or electronic contact. For those who don't see their customers, we tell them to *visualize* that they're looking into people's eyes as they speak to them over the phone or communicate through other electronic means.

Try to visualize what that person might look like, and then *mentally* look into the person's eyes. This helps cut out influences and distractions that might otherwise cause your mind to wander. When you accompany this physical act with the genuine attitude "Connecting with you is the most important thing I can do at this moment," you will communicate sincerity and genuine interest to that person.

Just this week I attended a graduation of our "The Customer" program with a large insurance company. One of the graduates explained how learning to look "through the telephone" into someone's eyes helped her totally focus on her customers. She mentioned that before she'd been listening halfheartedly, checking her e-mail with one eye and noticing passersby with the other—not giving the person she was talking to her full attention.

When she changed her focus, her rapport with other people immediately improved, as did her own confidence and sense of personal power. As a result she not only served customers more effectively but also enjoyed doing it more.

Thank Them for Coming In or Contacting You

This sounds so simple, and really it is, but analyze the performance of the next ten service people you encounter—I'll bet very few of them do it. Most people move immediately to the "What can I do for you?" or "How can I help you?" approach.

They leave out this important step.

The people at the Ritz-Carlton Hotels don't leave it out. They're well trained, so that from your first contact with telephone answerers, registration hosts, or baggage handlers, you get a "Thank you for calling (or choosing) the Ritz-Carlton Hotel."

The Ritz-Carlton in Phoenix knows that good customer service is a value, not a strategy, and managers interview twenty people in order to find one who fits their criteria. They carefully observe potential job candidates to see if they have the skill of enjoying people. Are they naturally friendly? They want people who can look past the work they do and remember the real reason why they do it—to give customer satisfaction. Their motto is, *We are ladies and gentlemen serving ladies and gentlemen.*

Employees demonstrate this credo in all their contacts with

customers and other associates. They feel special, which, of course, fills one of their own greatest needs as individuals.

Effective people know that helping guests, patients, or customers feel special begins by honestly viewing them as special. This behavior is driven by the internal values of individuals. It's not just a strategy; when we honestly think customers are special, we'll communicate that to them.

I was in one of our client's offices recently and noticed a name plate on the reception desk. It had the receptionist's name and then the title: *Director of First Impressions.*

In a sense, all of us who serve other people should claim this title, because first impressions are so important for successful customer communications.

Tune the World Out and Them In

Another effective service behavior is to tune the world out and patients, clients, members, guests, or customers in. Good communicators have learned to break their own preoccupation. They notice people. They tune into them.

In a seminar I did once for dental staff and doctors, someone told me a story about preoccupation. He said he'd recently acquired a new patient, and upon querying the person about why she decided to come to his office and leave the one she had been going to, he learned something rather interesting.

It seemed that when the woman had last visited her regular dentist, he had something new. When she was seated in the office, the dentist came in with a headset on. It had an earphone and a spiral cord that trailed down through his belt loop and dangled there.

As he came into the operatory, he washed his hands, routinely spoke to her, and began his work. Upon doing this, he plugged the spiral cord into a telephone jack and began a conversation with his stockbroker while examining the patient. It wasn't exactly a warm experience for the patient, and needless to say, she was underwhelmed.

The dentist had probably been to a recent time-management seminar and thought he was making the best use of his time. Or maybe he was just bored at having to look into people's mouths. Whatever the case, it definitely cost him at least one patient who took her mouth and checkbook to some other dental office.

Now, you say, "Oh, come on. I would never be that blatant." And, of course, you probably wouldn't. But how often do we mentally talk to our stockbrokers when we should be focusing on our customers? It's called preoccupation. Preoccupation is thinking about something else rather than about the people in our here and now. It's very easy to do unconsciously and can be very damaging to our customer relations.

In the last few years we've been introduced to the term "multitasking." Bosses love it. Customers are often turned off by it. The problem is that a human being can focus on only one thing at a time. You can't truly listen to and focus on customers while reading or deleting your e-mail. You can't totally listen to one person while waving to all the people who pass by your workstation.

In our high-tech world, it's too easy to try to do three things at once, but when you do this, usually they all receive your unfocused attention. When it comes to serving your external or internal associates, try "single-tasking" it. Do *one* thing. Focus on the people with whom you're communicating.

All of us have been the recipients of someone's partial attention while they check their computer or talk to a friend on their cell phone. That behavior does not say to us, "Understanding and satisfying you is the most important thing I can do with my time at this moment."

What disturbs your focus with people? What is an appropriate focus?

Do You Have a Process Focus or a People Focus?

As I've observed people at work, I've noticed that they have either a *process focus* or a *people focus*.

Here's the difference:

- Process focus—*"I'm here to do my job."*
- People focus—*"I'm here to serve customers and associates."*

You may be in a bookstore, where a clerk asks you to move so he can restock the shelf. Or in a department store, a hotel, or another place where people's actions tell you "My first responsibility is to do my job well, fill in the forms correctly, or make my cash drawer balance; then I'll attend to you."

I don't want to seem too harsh about this. I know there are many conscientious people whose main goal is to do their jobs well. Maybe they've never been taught that there's a higher purpose for their jobs. That higher purpose would be to satisfy and keep loyal customers.

My experience is that when people understand this *purpose* and, consequently, the need for a *customer focus*, they develop a new attitude or feeling of importance.

I clearly remember getting a letter from a bank teller who was enrolled in one of our courses. She described an elderly woman who came to her window each month to deposit her Social Security check. The customer was always dressed up and seemed to want to visit longer than most other customers did.

One month when the woman came in, the teller informed her about a new drive-up window and how it might be more convenient for her to deposit her check there rather than coming into the bank.

When the teller said this, the woman frowned, shook her head, and said, "Oh, no, I would never want to do that." She then told the teller a story that really astounded her.

The customer said that she lived on the outskirts of the city, had been widowed for several years, and had no family or close neighbors. The only time she came to town was once a month to deposit her check. She looked forward to her visit, planning what she was going to wear several days in advance.

The customer then told the bank teller that the teller was her best friend.

The teller was stunned. She had had no idea. She concluded her letter by saying that this incident completely changed her view of her job. Instead of seeing it as balancing her cash drawer and being efficient, she now saw it as a chance to touch people.

She went from having a *process focus* to having a *people focus*, and her job took on more meaning for her.

What's the Payoff for Having a Customer Focus?

There is an unerring law of human action—*the law of psychological reciprocity*. It means that in our interactions with people, we *usually get back what we give out*. When we give *psychological value* to people, they're *instinctively* impelled to reciprocate by returning this value back to us. They do it by being receptive, more attentive, more open, and less guarded.

We all know this law on an instinctual level. Give someone a smile, and you'll usually get one back. Show concern for people's needs, and they'll most often show concern for you. Yell at someone, and he'll usually yell back.

When people receive positive responses, this law can cause an emotional bond to quickly form, where each person feels good about the other. As a consequence, both feel reinforced or energized. They feel an affinity, or connection, that sets the stage for successful further transactions. Let me emphasize that this happens on an instinctual level, not just a conscious one.

Mutual attraction, or psychological reciprocity, happens as we value people and treat them with dignity and respect. The opposite happens when we're rude or brusque with people — they return those behaviors to us.

Every individual has what I'll call an *attraction potential*. It's the degree to which we're able to attract other people. Call it winning friends or influencing people. It's our unique ability to cause others to feel comfortable around us, to feel good about or be attracted to us.

One other important point — this universal law works in proportion to the motives that drive our external behaviors. If we act with the objective of getting responses we want from others, mutual attraction loses much of its power. But if we act because valuing people is a *value* we have, the power of mutual attraction is heightened. Its effect is directly proportionate to the sincerity with which we act.

In a sense, this law works according to what William James called "The Law of Reverse Effect." Here's its meaning:

> The less we try to impress others, and the more we attempt to understand them, our power of mutual attraction increases. It's a hard and fast fact of life that the more we focus on giving value to others, the more they'll be instinctively impelled to return that value to us.

Paradoxically, our self-esteem is enhanced when we view our jobs as focusing on and creating value for people. There's a built-in positive reciprocity in the very act of doing this.

To be genuinely interested in creating value for other people brings its own rewards of greater confidence and a sense of importance. Job satisfaction, the joy of work, and personal happiness are enhanced as we tune into the uniqueness and wonder of each person we meet. The great writer Tolstoy wrote, "Joy can be real only if people look upon their life as a service, and have a definite object in life outside themselves and their personal happiness."

Not Everyone Thinks or Sees the World as You Do

Aren't you constantly amazed at how people think so differently? How can two people view the world so differently? How can another person see the same set of "facts" as you, yet interpret them in a vastly dissimilar way?

It seems that we all view life through different-colored lenses. Our experiences, education, and acquired perceptions cause us to think in various patterns. The "Behavior Styles Model" shown here will help you understand the diverse ways people think, act, and respond.

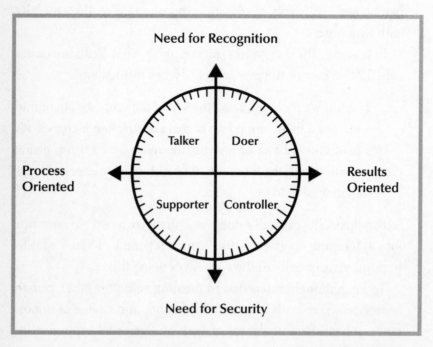

Behavior Styles Model

We'll apply this model throughout these chapters, as it relates to different communication skills. Let's take a quick look at how you might identify each style in your initial contacts.

Doers show high energy, confidence, and authority. They want you to notice them for their power and achievement. They can appear flashy or demanding.

Controllers are logical, no-nonsense people who value accuracy, efficiency, and good organization. They want you to listen to and thoroughly understand them. They can first appear very critical.

Supporters are steady, stable, salt-of-the-earth people. They value security and safety, and they carefully avoid risks. They'll appear compliant and nonassertive.

Talkers are affable, friendly, social people. They want you to be their friend and show interest in them, their activities, and their families. They'll be easy to approach as long as you allow them to do most of the talking.

As you learn more about behavior styles, you'll be able to identify *your* and your customers' styles, as well as how you'll naturally interact.

HOW TO GAIN THE MOST FROM THIS CHAPTER

As you review this chapter, don't be fooled by the simplicity of my suggestions. They may sound mushy when you only read them, but they become dynamic and life-changing when practiced.

Few things cause customers to enjoy a lift more than when we look at them and communicate a genuine feeling of "You've just made my day by coming in or contacting me!"

Paradoxically, the recipient of this joy usually sends it back to the giver, which then helps make your day brighter.

Please keep the following thoughts in mind as you go through this week.

1. *A lot of selling or communication takes place during the first few seconds of contact you have with your customers. Feelings and perceptions are quickly formed and are often lasting ones.*

2. *Your eye contact, your attitude, and your ability to break away from preoccupations, tuning the world out and the person in, have immediate impact on people. This can't be explained with logic; it all happens emotionally. Your nonverbal gestures, body language, and facial expressions make quick subliminal impressions on people.*

3. *When you make the best first impression, customers are going to say to themselves "I like this person," "I feel good about this person," and "I want to do business here." When you don't make a good first impression, they may subconsciously say to themselves, "I don't feel comfortable here," "This person isn't really interested in me," or "This isn't a place where I want to do business."*

4. *Your actions will largely determine which of these responses you receive.*

Yes, it all begins with the way you *greet* people. So much happens in the first few seconds. Your sincerity, genuine interest in people, excitement with who you are and what you do—these are the causes that produce the effects of putting people at ease and making them feel welcome.

Take a few moments and fill in the following Self-Assessment. It's designed to cause you to think about some very practical, yet important, skills, values, and attitudes. You may even want to write some of these statements on an index card, or on your screen saver, as a reminder to practice them.

Also, please fill in the Daily Success Diary, and evaluate your performance each day. Seek to improve each day.

Go out and do your own research. Check out places where you spend money. See how little these common courtesies are done. Then notice how great you feel when someone greets you properly. Pay attention to how you feel when people say with their actions, "Hey, you're the customer . . . You pay my salary! I'm here to serve you!"

Self-Assessment: *Greet Customers*

Take a moment to read each of the following statements. Then circle the number that best describes your actions or thoughts, with *1* being "Never" and *10* being "Always."

1. I see my job as mainly serving customers or associates.

   1   2   3   4   5   6   7   8   9   10

2. At each moment of contact, I focus totally on the customer.

   1   2   3   4   5   6   7   8   9   10

3. I view each person as having unique needs.

   1   2   3   4   5   6   7   8   9   10

4. I always cause people to feel special when I come in contact with them.

   1   2   3   4   5   6   7   8   9   10

5. I always want people to feel good about themselves when I approach them.

   1   2   3   4   5   6   7   8   9   10

6. Regardless of what I'm doing, I consciously refocus on people when I contact them.

   1   2   3   4   5   6   7   8   9   10

7. I believe that people return the same responses to me as I give them.

   1   2   3   4   5   6   7   8   9   10

8. I have learned that a smile and friendly greeting usually cause people to reciprocate.

   1   2   3   4   5   6   7   8   9   10

9. I believe that building others' self-confidence helps build my own.

   1   2   3   4   5   6   7   8   9   10

10. I always try to make the most of my first ten seconds of contact with a person.

   1   2   3   4   5   6   7   8   9   10

Action Guide: *Daily Success Diary* ✐ ✎

Greet Customers

Please score yourself from 1 to 10 for each daily activity, with
1 being "Never" and *10* being "Always."

	S	M	T	W	T	F	S
1. I consciously valued the value of valuing each person today.							
2. I made eye contact with each person whom I encountered.							
3. I thanked each person for contacting me or for coming in.							
4. I tuned the world out and people in.							
5. I saw evidence of practicing the law of psychological reciprocity today.							
6. I kept a people focus rather than a process focus today.							
Total each day							

I have brought myself, by long meditation, to the conviction that a human being with a settled purpose must accomplish it, and that nothing can resist a will which will stake even existence upon its fulfillment. (Benjamin Disraeli)

3 Identify Purpose

Choose What to Do with Your Life

One of the graduates of our "The Customer" course worked in the cafeteria of Holmes Regional Medical Center in Melbourne, Florida, making Jell-O. Day in and day out, she made Jell-O. Upon enrolling in our program, she had to introduce herself to her group and tell what she did in the hospital. Hanging her head, looking at the floor, she said quietly, "I work in the cafeteria, making Jell-O."

Her words revealed her low belief in the value of *what* she did and, sadly, *who* she was.

In the eight weeks of our course, she set goals each week and reported her results to her group. She received lots of positive reinforcement and encouragement. People sent her encouraging notes during the weeks; she was given unconditional acceptance by her facilitator and other course participants. She began to internalize the positive words her course members mentioned about her, and when she felt it safe to do so, she moved out of herself and began focusing on others. The eighth session was a graduation where all the participants, in turn, stood and shared what they'd gained from the course, how they'd applied it, and how they would continue to practice the course concepts in the future.

When the cafeteria worker's turn came to speak, she stood, beaming, and said, "What I've gained from this course is to realize that I make people happy. Do you realize how it makes people happier to eat Jell-O?" she asked. "You ever watch little kids eat Jell-O? They love it. They like to look at it. They like to swish it around in their mouths. I've started noticing how elderly patients love my Jell-O. I get a kick out of finding out why they like different colors. I love to see older patients enjoy my Jell-O, when that's all they can eat."

She was just getting wound up. "You realize how many flavors of Jell-O there are? There's strawberry, cherry, lime, lemon . . ." She went on listing all the exciting flavors.

She concluded by saying, "I can't think of a more exciting job that I could have. I just get up every morning knowing that I'm gonna make a lot of people happy today, and . . . that makes me happy!"

Wow! What a transformation.

She'd discovered a significant secret that many people never find in their jobs or careers—*purpose*.

What Is a Purpose?

A purpose is a well-thought-out life direction. It's what I want to *do* with my life. It's choosing what I give my life *to*—*why* I do what I do. It infuses meaning into what I do. We can have both a *life* purpose and a *job* or *career* purpose.

The nineteenth-century naturalist John Burroughs wrote, "A man's life may stay stagnant as literally as water may stagnate, and just as motion and direction are the remedy for one, so purpose and activity are the remedy for the other."

On a higher level, the Belgian writer Maurice Maeterlinck once observed, "Each man has to seek out his own special aptitude for a higher life in the midst of the humble and inevitable reality of daily existence."

Some people choose their purpose; others just settle for what comes along.

Having a Purpose Transforms Your Life

Like the beautiful spirit who found her purpose in the *joys of Jell-O*, you too will experience a transformation as your focus moves past *what* you do to *why* you do it.

Taking it deeper—here's what I believe to be the truth:

1. *The more your purpose is self-focused, the less real joy and happiness you'll experience.*
2. *The more your purpose is to contribute to and enhance the lives of others, the more genuine joy and happiness you'll experience.*

Herein lies one of the greatest of life's mental, emotional, and spiritual challenges: *Should I follow my own self-focused way, or choose to look past my own ego needs and focus on how I can create value for others?* The following illustration shows the seesaw that goes on within us.

Paradoxically, the more I focus on filling *your* needs, the

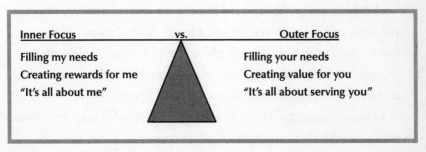

Inner Focus	vs.	Outer Focus
Filling my needs		Filling your needs
Creating rewards for me		Creating value for you
"It's all about me"		"It's all about serving you"

The Focus Challenge

more *my* needs become filled. This eternal truth remains well-hidden in plain sight and only materializes in our awareness as our values drive our behaviors in that direction. It is only through serious searching that we gain the wisdom to truly understand this paradox.

Okay, I know that none of us is perfect, so let's cut ourselves a little slack here, and admit that we're all in a state of growth. Let's relax a bit and take a fresh look at our own lives and the purposes of them.

What's the Purpose of Your Life and Career?

We come now to the main question of this chapter: *What is your purpose?* What can you do, or are you doing, to use your talents to contribute to the lives of others?

With all sincerity and conviction, I believe that the way you answer these questions will influence your future happiness, your sense of meaning, and your career success. If you agree with me, then you've just taken responsibility for your success in a way that few people do. If you're ready, the rest of this chapter will help you sort through a thinking process to arrive at a definition of your life and career purposes.

Selecting Your Career Purpose

While you'll probably want to define a higher purpose for your life than just your career, let's first focus on that aspect, since customer service is the primary objective of this book. Let me emphasize this: *The starting point of all successful achievement is the adoption of a definite purpose and a plan to carry it out.*

Here are some questions to ask yourself. Record your responses on a separate sheet if you need more space.

1. What jobs, activities, or functions do you enjoy the most?

_____

2. What do people who know you say your talents are?

_____

3. Who do you serve in your job?

_____

4. What specific value do you create for your customers or internal associates?

_____

5. What specific incidents in your life caused you to feel more alive and good about yourself?

_____

6. What extra-mile efforts have you made in the past?

_____

7. What differentiates you from other people who do what you do?

_____

8. What greater value can you create for people than you're currently doing?

_____

Please reflect upon these questions.

Here's a truth I believe: Those who show up on their jobs merely to get through the day will eventually be replaced by people who have a clearly defined purpose. Those who come to work to do a good job will continue to receive basically the same compensation. Those who see their jobs as creating value for their customers, associates, or organizations will always be sought out, and their compensation will be expanded time and again—depending on the actual value they do create.

Granted, this belief conflicts with many people's attitude: *Give me more pay for less work.* But in a free country, all of us have the clear choice of which career view we adopt. This will be a choice you make. But be assured that you'll set in motion certain predetermined results with your decision.

Your conscious or unconscious choice will become your guiding purpose, and whatever it is will motivate certain actions . . . and predictable career results.

Defining Your Career Purpose

After you've thought about the previous eight questions and arrived at some answers, you're ready to move to the next step. Now, it's time to put pen to paper and write out your career purpose. Here's an example.

The major purpose of my position of _____ is to:

1. Help attract and/or keep loyal, satisfied customers by giving them the following extra value.

   _____

2. Help teammates and associates become more productive by giving them the following support and encouragement.

   _____

3. Help my organization enjoy greater growth and profitability in the following ways.

   _____

Once you've clearly defined your own purpose, specifically stated to fit these three areas, visit with a manager, an associate, or a trusted friend. Solicit that person's advice. Ask for the person's ideas about the eight previous questions. When you've arrived at your best answers for now, consider writing them out on a card or using electronic means.

Don't reveal or talk about your career purpose to anyone who'll react negatively or feel threatened by your increased success. My experience tells me that you'll rewrite your career purpose statements several times as you follow my instructions about how to actualize them.

Remember that you can always revise or restate your purpose as your goals, opportunities, or self-beliefs change—as they will once you begin this process. So be flexible enough to deal with changes around you, as well as your own personal growth.

Write Out Clear Plans

After you've defined your purpose in the three previous career categories, you'll need to put action steps to each one. Keep things simple at this point; think of actions you can take now to move toward your purpose.

Remember that your purpose is the reason for what you do. It isn't simply a goal—goals are milestones that lay out how you fulfill your purpose.

After reflecting on your three areas of career purpose, please write down your response to actions you'll take. Fill in the blanks below or use a separate pad.

1. Actions I will take to give customers extra value:

a. _____

_____

b. _____

_____

c. _____

_____

2. Actions I will take to help my teammates be more productive:

a. _____

_____

b. _____

_____

c. _____

_____

3. Actions I will take to help my organization enjoy greater growth and profitability:

a. _____

_____

b. _____

_____

c. _____

_____

Gain New Purpose

After you've written your purpose in the three areas and put legs to them by writing action statements, you can take steps to gain new levels of confidence, belief, and enthusiasm.

Here's how to do this.

1. *Transfer each of your three statements of purpose to index cards. Write your purpose statement and action steps for each purpose.*
2. *Carry these cards with you, referring to them several times each day.*
   a. *Read them.*
   b. *Visualize yourself achieving each purpose.*
3. *Welcome and get excited about taking the action steps, thinking about the rewards they'll bring you.*
4. *When you've carried out your action steps, give yourself a daily and weekly reward for your successful practice.*

Remember—it's the hope of rewards that motivates you to do the necessary activities that cause you to excel in your career, so carefully select rewards that will excite and energize you.

More than a hundred years ago James Allen, writing in his classic *As a Man Thinketh*, penned these words about the power of purpose: "Thought allied with purpose becomes creative force." The fact is that until we are guided and motivated by the saturation of purpose, we'll suffer career limitations. Said more positively, when our minds are focused on our career purpose, we'll

- *have more energy,*
- *discover new levels of creativity,*
- *enjoy a heightened desire to learn,*
- *make decisions easier,*
- *be strongly motivated to reach goals,* and
- *enjoy our jobs more.*

Without a clear purpose there's no reason to learn, grow, or take risks. There's no *why* in our lives—no set of our sails. Any breeze can blow us off course. Any adversity can send us in several different directions. The slightest problem can discourage us. Without purpose, our work has little or no meaning. We fail to savor significance in what we do.

But with purpose, we bask in zest, challenge, meaning, and aliveness. We're able to deal with the ultimate setbacks that everyone experiences. We welcome periodic ups and downs as only temporary zigzag lines to reaching our goals.

Purpose Helps Us Deal with Adversity

I can promise you that your life isn't going to be an episode of smooth sailing, devoid of problems, challenges, or setbacks. Shakespeare wrote so eloquently about life's uncertainties with these words: "The heartache and the thousand natural shocks that flesh is heir to . . ."

Having observed many people in their careers and life pursuits, I've found that few have the emotional tensile strength to stand and fight when things go bad. Most bolt and run to apparent greener pastures, only to find that there are no safe havens that are problem-free. The pastures on the other side of the fence are usually the same color.

So much of success is having the emotional durability to keep going when the going gets tough. This enduring attitude only infuses us when we're guided by a noble purpose.

The German philosopher Nietzsche observed, "He who has a *why* to live can bear almost any *how*."

Purpose is the *why*. It gives meaning to the *what* we do and helps us manage the *how* of temporary life circumstances.

Your Purpose Must Be Aligned with Your Values

Your purpose must be congruent with, driven by, and sustained by your values. Your values are *who* you *are* and create the boundaries of your actual behaviors. The strength of your purpose will be inextricably linked to the intensity of your commitment to your values. A noble, service-driven purpose that's inconsistent with a person's values will eventually cause self-destruction, because it's not built on a firm foundation.

The business purpose of my organization, Integrity Systems, is to help organizations and individuals enjoy higher levels of personal growth, customer loyalty, and profitability. Obviously, with a firm name like *Integrity*, we have a higher level of expectations for our associates. I once had a senior executive who could eloquently spout the values of honesty and integrity as success factors in business. Then one day, I caught him faking sales and paying himself commissions and bonuses. How he thought he could get by with this practice on a long-term basis is beyond me. But obviously he thought he could. Or maybe he was motivated by financial pressures. Either way, he lacked the personal integrity that he so nobly expounded to potential clients.

His values were out of congruence with our corporate purpose.

Your Career Purpose Must Be Congruent with Your Life Purpose

You are *mind, body, spirit. Brain, heart, soul.* You *think*, you *feel*, you *are*.

If you have only a career purpose, you'll ultimately discover an emptiness that leaches out your overall sense of worth, happiness, and meaning. Workaholics bear this out, and brokenness is left in their wake. Their exteriors and success trappings thinly veil a deeper emptiness.

Our intellectual and emotional dimensions don't exist apart from our spiritual selves. We can't achieve balance if one or two dimensions are filled without a third one also being addressed.

My life's purpose transcends what I do. *What* I do doesn't have the most weight in determining *why* I'm here on this planet at this time. There are deeper, more profound reasons why I'm here than how I do my job. My career purpose, while important to my material and emotional well-being, isn't the ultimate good to which I should give my life. To reach the deepest recesses of my being, I must of necessity consider the essence of who I am, and my overriding purpose.

If my overriding purpose in life is to *seek the highest good for other people*, then how do I go about this in my individual life? Is this the Supreme Good—the *summum bonum?* Is this the noblest act that we can do each day? Could this be the hidden pathway to a happy life?

The question of the ages is this: If we but practice this one virtue—*seeking the highest good for others*—would we inadvertently practice all the other appropriate social graces? Would this value guide and ensure our success with people? Would it serendipitously ensure our success with ourselves?

All these questions call for answers and/or choices we'll either consciously or unconsciously make. We'll make them by direct action or by default. But make them we will!

It's not my intent with this customer service book to tell you what your choices should be, but rather to encourage you to ask yourself these questions. I do know that temporary goals will not be substantially supported unless you first answer your life purpose and make your goals and your purpose congruent.

Rick Warren, writing in his runaway bestseller, *The Purpose-Driven Life*, makes a simple point: "Focusing on ourselves will never reveal our life's purpose." We don't find our life's purpose by placing ourselves at the center of our search—despite what people might tell you. A self-focus blinds us to the Supreme Purpose to which we should give our lives.

Filter Your Decisions and Choices Through Your Career and Life Purpose

A well-defined purpose gives you clarity of direction in the decisions and choices you make or goals you set. When your purpose is right, and your choices are congruent with it, you have personal power, as illustrated in the following diagram.

This interaction helps reveal your character—the *who* that you are. Where harmony exists within this inner state, you do well. You have confidence, energy, and a feeling of well-being. Ulti-

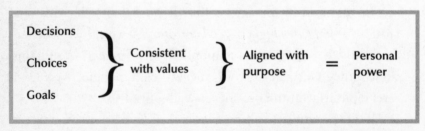

Personal Power Convergence Model

mately, your life circumstances are the result of this inner state. James Allen, in *As a Man Thinketh*, makes this point: "Men are anxious to improve their circumstances, but are unwilling to improve themselves; they therefore remain bound."

This hundred-year-old wisdom is just as true today as it was when Allen wrote it. Maybe it's needed in this present time more than ever.

Achieving an inner congruence often forces you to make difficult choices. It's so easy to bend the rules a little this way or that way in order to get ahead. But there's always a compensation for our choices. Payment may come quickly, or it may take time. It may affect you outwardly or inwardly, but you predetermine the ultimate payback with your initial choices and actions.

A business consultant friend recently told me of a very difficult decision he had to make. It involved working with an organization whose values weren't aligned with those of its CEO. My friend was called in to help with their strategic planning. After sizing up the organization's situation and stated goals, he visited with many people within the organization who told him many times that the CEO's values were not congruent with the stated values of the organization—nor with theirs.

Confronting the CEO with his lifestyle, my friend told him that the whole planning project wouldn't work unless the CEO changed his actions, policies, and dictatorial style. The response he got was "I've been here too long and am too set in my ways to change now."

"Okay," my friend told him, "then I can't help you, and whatever you'd pay me would be wasted."

My friend walked away from a multimillion-dollar contract.

"How did you feel?" I asked.

"Poorer," he joked. "But I did the right thing, and the right thing is the right thing."

You probably won't have to make decisions of this size every day, but any decision to act in congruence with your values and purpose is the right decision.

Personal Growth and Education Must Have a Purpose

Learning and personal growth must be aligned with your purposes in order to have meaning. Growth without a purpose is self-focused and can even be narcissistic and directed toward the outer package rather than toward the inner being. When our reason for learning or personal growth is just to know, we can miss the mark. We are misled if we think knowledge alone is power. Knowledge applied toward positive goals produces power.

I take issue with many personal growth processes that exist today. Many teach "nurture yourself," which, in my opinion, can lead people into the wrong direction of being self-absorbed. Ironically, this self-focus can steer people into ruts of low self-esteem, because they have a misguided purpose. As they sink into the quicksand of self-absorption, they individually lose their real selves rather than *finding* the who that they are.

High self-esteem is invariably developed as a process of serving and creating value for others. Nurtured selves is the serendipity that happens when we nurture others. Our very being is nurtured as we extend ourselves for the purpose of creating value for others.

This is life's great mystery that lies undiscovered by many people, because we look up the wrong avenues for finding true joy, happiness, and meaning.

In our three-dimensional language, when our purpose of growth is to equip ourselves to create value for others, and when we feel worthy to receive a reciprocal benefit, our "*I Am*" is nourished. This inner feeling then powerfully produces an emotional affluence that bubbles up to make our careers more fulfilling.

Choose your purpose carefully, because in choosing it, you'll select your quality of life.

HOW TO GAIN THE MOST FROM THIS CHAPTER

Purpose is choosing what to do with your life—*what to give it to.* People with stated purposes have personal power that others don't have. They steer a clearer course. They don't make a lot of false moves or detours. People to whom fate seems to direct special smiles are people who are guided by a clear purpose.

A purpose is not a goal. It's a life direction. Goals help us carry out our purposes.

While this chapter's main concern has been to help you clarify your career purpose, an even more important one is your *life's purpose.*

To gain the most from this chapter, reread it and then perhaps write on index cards stated career purposes and actions you'll take to carry them out.

I suggest that you think of your job purpose as

1. *helping attract and/or keep loyal customers;*
2. *helping teammates and associates become more productive by giving them support and encouragement;*
3. *helping your organization enjoy greater growth and profitability.*

The extent to which you carry out these purposes will determine your value to your organization—and often your compensation.

Write these statements on cards, filling in the specific ways you'll create value, and then write actions you'll take to carry out these purposes.

Carry these cards with you. Read them several times each day, and you'll soon begin to stand out from your associates and catch the attention of your managers as a special person.

Also, I sincerely encourage you to define your major life purpose. This becomes the emotional and spiritual steering mechanism to lead you to your other purposes—as they are congruent with it.

Self-Assessment: *Identify Purpose* ✐ ✎

Take a moment to read each of the following statements. Then circle the number that best describes your actions or thoughts, with *1* being "Never" and *10* being "Always."

1. I clearly see my job as a vehicle for serving others.

    1   2   3   4   5   6   7   8   9   10

2. I have a well-defined, written purpose statement for my career.

    1   2   3   4   5   6   7   8   9   10

3. I know that success is a by-product of serving others.

    1   2   3   4   5   6   7   8   9   10

4. My values are congruent with my stated purpose.

    1   2   3   4   5   6   7   8   9   10

5. Before I make decisions, I review my purpose.

    1   2   3   4   5   6   7   8   9   10

6. I also have a well-defined life purpose.

    1   2   3   4   5   6   7   8   9   10

7. I read and update my action steps to carry out my purpose each day.

    1   2   3   4   5   6   7   8   9   10

8. I spend time daily saturating my mind with my purpose.

    1   2   3   4   5   6   7   8   9   10

9. I review my purpose to help me move through problems and decisions.

    1   2   3   4   5   6   7   8   9   10

10. I am content to be compensated according to the value I create for others.

    1   2   3   4   5   6   7   8   9   10

I can live two months on a good compliment. (Mark Twain)

4 Value Customers

View Everyone as a Creative Person
Who Enriches Your Life

It was 1970 when I was escorted by a friend into Elliott's Hardware in Dallas, Texas. Jerre Elliott, the owner, was at the front door to greet everyone. He'd been involved in one of my courses, and with his great, effusive smile and warm handshake, he made me feel as though I was the most important person to ever stroll into his store.

I spent time in his small store talking to employees and customers. The parking lot was jammed with every kind of car you can imagine—from Volkswagens to Rolls-Royces. Jerre called most of the people who came in by their first names—from Tom Landry to Ross Perot.

His friendliness and warmth all communicated these sentiments:

- *"You've made my day by coming in!"*
- *"You're the customer—you pay my salary!"*
- *"There's something about you that I like!"*
- *"We're here on your account!"*
- *"We're here to serve you!"*

For two or three hours, I witnessed people enjoy a most unusual experience—one far different than they'd have had at other hardware stores. They felt valued. It was as if they were going to a movie, or an entertainment event, not just going to buy hardware.

Fast-forward thirty-four years.

Recently, I noticed a two-page article about Elliott's in *The Dallas Morning News*. It started by saying "If you need to find a thingamajig to fix your whatchamacallit or one of those plastic strap-like doohickeys the guys at Elliott's can fix you right up."

The story went on to tell about employees like Carl Williams, Ken Kerges, and Jim Bennett, who greet customers and cause them to feel special with handshakes, hugs, and friendly greetings. Their largest location is 74,000 square feet—quite a bit different from the small store I first went into. Today they have three locations and seven greeters. They greet everyone entering with "Hello" and "How may I help you?"

Most of the greeters are retired—an ex-Olympic boxer, a car salesman, a printer, and a banker, among others. "I'll be here until I can't put one foot in front of another," one greeter said. Another, a retired mortgage banker, at sixty-seven is called "the new kid" on the job. He said, "I meet someone who says 'I have this broken so-and-so,' and that gets me out of thinking about mortgage banking."

One customer came in with a broken doorknob, not knowing how to fix it. He showed it to a clerk, who took time to explain how to repair it, showed him a tool that would help him, and answered the customer's questions. The total sale was 39 cents, for an Allen wrench.

Elliott's CEO, Charlie Bond, said that an encyclopedic knowledge isn't a job requirement for a greeter. "They need to like people, and genuinely want to help them."

Yes, having greeters costs the store more, but Bond says it's what sets Elliott's apart. "If we didn't have them, we'd be just another hardware store."

A customer remarked, "You come here, you grab a guy, and he takes you right to it."

Customers feel valued at Elliott's. And this brings us to the second step on the *G. Val Hi* System: *Value customers*.

Valuing Customers Is a Value, Not a Strategy

A cousin of mine, a physician, told me of a sign in the surgeon's dressing room of a hospital where he saw patients: "In this hospital sincerity is the most important quality. If you don't have it, fake it!"

Well, obviously, the sign elicits a chuckle, but it also makes a serious point: Sincerity can't be faked. It must come from the hearts of people as a value. But sincere common courtesy isn't common in many industries.

Are you old enough to remember when passengers and travel-related workers were actually polite to each other? Yeah, I kinda thought you were probably too young to remember that. You gotta be pretty old to have experienced that kind of treatment.

The nonpartisan opinion organization Public Agenda and the online travel site Travelocity did a survey. It included 875 airline, bus, train, and highway workers, along with 1,009 Travelocity members. The survey found that these employees didn't always emulate Emily Post, but neither did the travelers.

Sixty-five percent of the passengers cited the rudeness of workers as a serious problem. But get this—more than half of the travel employees said that passenger rudeness was a major cause of their own job stress.

Do we have a problem here? Who's responsible?

Ruth Warden, president of Public Agenda, asked, "Is there a solution short of time travel to an earlier, kinder day?"

Her answer: "Although bad manners are contagious, good manners are, too. I would like to think if people were aware of this, they might take a second breath before lashing out."

Good Manners Are Contagious, Too

As we think of these statistics, it becomes obvious that not only can we control our own reactions to people, but our behaviors actually influence other people's responses to us. We're not only our own keeper, but to some degree we're also our brother's or sister's keeper. When we take responsibility for our own actions, we indirectly influence the actions of other people.

The question becomes "Am I willing to control my own actions and responses and act in a positive, professional manner, regardless of how other people with whom I interact choose to act?"

Making these choices assumes the following beliefs and values:

- *"I'm responsible for my own actions."*
- *"Often my actions and reactions influence those of other people with whom I interact."*
- *"Other people's actions and responses are their choices and will not negatively influence mine."*

In other words: If you choose to rain on my parade, I'm still gonna keep enjoying the sunshine!

We each make our own choices. The question remains this: *Who controls my choices?* If your answer is "me," then go to the head of the line. You're going to get a gold star on your attendance chart today.

The Law of Psychological Reciprocity

We come again to a natural law of human action. Remember? It's this: *People are instinctively motivated to return to us the attitudes, feelings, and behaviors that we give them.*

Please read that again. It's true, isn't it?

When people are courteous to us, we return that to them. When they're rude to us, we instinctively deliver the same response back to them.

"But," you ask, "what about those surly, mean-spirited people who aren't influenced by my courtesy? After all, it's a dog-eat-dog, shark-infested world out there. Everyone's out to take advantage of me!"

Hey, I know there are people like that, but that's their problem. If I've attempted to give value to them and they don't accept it, I've done all I can do. I won't allow them to spoil my day by transferring their negative attitude to me. Actually, it's these people who need my positive responses—probably more than others do.

Let's assume that what I'm sharing with you is only 85 percent true—that roughly 15 percent of all people choose not to value us or treat us with dignity or respect. Allow that to be their problem, not yours or mine.

The law of psychological reciprocity gives us a values-focused framework with which to treat other people. For all practical purposes this is the Golden Rule, operating as a dynamic law of human interaction. And it's my belief that it works with most people.

Even the surliest of people melt when a two-year-old smiles and hugs them, and says, "I wuv you." Most of us are touched, reached, and motivated when we receive psychological value.

Giving Psychological Value

Any student of human behavior soon discovers that one of the strongest motivators of people is the need to be valued, understood, and noticed—that is, to receive *psychological value*.

Psychological value is communicated both consciously and unconsciously. Its persuasive power primarily operates through the instinctive levels of people. Most of us respond involuntarily to the actions and attitudes of others.

I learned this as a young office equipment salesman many years ago. I was calling on purchasing agents and office managers and was green as a Saint Patrick's Day parade. I remember calling on John Ketler, who was president of a savings and loan institution.

Mr. Ketler was a short, small person with a cigar and a bark as big as that of a Saint Bernard. The first time I called on him, I only got within twenty feet of his office. He saw me coming with a catalog case, obviously sniffed me out as a salesman, and yelled out, "We don't want anything!"

I was totally embarrassed, knowing that the other twenty or so people around him were laughing under their breath at me. I felt as low as a mole's navel and wished I could immediately evaporate.

I was told to call on him every two weeks. Each time before I could even get to his office, I got the same response: "We don't want anything." If someone had given me the option of either calling on him or having my knees broken with a baseball bat, I would've, without blinking, chosen the latter.

One day I was driving around and saw a vacant lot for sale that I thought might make some money. "Who can give me some advice?" I wondered.

Mr. Ketler!

So I called him to see if I could come by and talk to him about it. Before I could tell him what I wanted, he barked out, "We don't want anything!"

"Yes, sir, I know that. I'm not trying to sell you anything. I want to ask your advice about a piece of property."

"A piece of property?" he asked, with some degree of caution. "Where?"

I told him. There was a pause. He suddenly changed his tune and said, "Come on by."

I did. He welcomed me into his office and for about an hour gave me some good advice. Then he asked me if I'd like to get a cup of coffee, which, of course, I did. Anything to kill time and keep me from calling on other people like him.

It wasn't long before he was buying lots of furniture, equipment, and supplies from me. He'd even call me at home at night and ask me to come to his office the next day. I think he must have worked twenty-four hours a day.

He turned out to be a loyal customer, and a person I greatly respected. I gave him psychological value by asking for his advice. In return he gave me lots of business, as well as his personal friendship.

Remember, most people are *instinctively* motivated to return to us the same value we give them.

How Do We Give Psychological Value?

When our behavior is sincerely motivated to give psychological value to people—not for the desired response, but because that's who we are—we get the best results. Every solid relationship is characterized by a mutual exchange of value that's being communicated back and forth. You give customers what they want—value. They then give you what you want—their business.

The same is true in our personal interactions.

Let me stress that *perceived value* is the strongest motivator of people. There are many kinds of perceived value. It could be giving customers more tangible value in your products or services than they expect. Or it could be that your recognizing and valuing them separates you from other vendors or providers.

Being genuinely interested in them, wanting to learn from

them, or asking for their advice or opinions shows value to people.

In a moment I'll share some more specific actions you can take to give people psychological value. First, though, let me suggest three *values* or *beliefs* that, if you sincerely possess them, you'll own the proper ethical foundation to complete the actions.

1. Think *"You're the customer—you pay my salary!"*
2. Think *"There's something about you I like!"*
3. Think *"You make my job possible!"*

If you're ever in Phoenix and want to have a superb dining experience, go to T. Cooks at the Royal Palms Hotel and Resort at 5200 East Camelback Road. You'll be greeted by Paul Xanthopoulos, the maitre d'.

With his charming, understated, old-world manner, Paul will make you feel so special that you feel you can't wait to return. Then watch him as he interacts with other customers. His unobtrusive, sincere joy for his job speaks louder than any billboard could communicate.

Before you leave, ask for his card, which he'll give you, along with a big smile that says "Thank you for asking. You've made my day just by coming in." Under his name and the word *Maitre D'* is his chosen title—*Director of Romance.*

Paul becomes the single most memorable part of dining there. The food is excellent, but many places have excellent food. No other place has him.

The restaurant has won the following awards.

Andrew Harper's Hideaway Report, *"2001 Best Hotel Resort Restaurant in the World."*

Food & Wine magazine, 2000 *Restaurant Poll, July 2000, tied for "Best Restaurant" in Phoenix and Scottsdale.*

Gourmet magazine, *"America's Top Tables," Reader's Poll.*

When you go, tell Paul I sent you. That way he'll continue to seat me at a good table.

What Sticks Out with Your Customers?

When internal and external customers or people whom you serve have contact with you, what sticks out in their minds about the experience? How do you differentiate yourself, and the service you give, from other people and their behavior? How do you lavish value upon your customers?

Let's think of some practical ways you can give *psychological value* to others. Let's begin with some very simple communication behaviors.

1. Give a sincere smile—*whether in person, over the telephone, or by e-mail. When you're smiling, you also change your voice, mood, and other mannerisms. There's something magical about it.*

2. Get people talking and you listening. *This behavior makes the statement that you're interested in them. You'll emotionally connect much faster than when you're talking.*

3. Nod as you understand and approve of what people are saying—*even if you're talking over the telephone.*

4. Verbalize your understanding of them and their needs. *Responses like "I see," "I understand," "Thank you," and "I appreciate what you're saying" reinforce to people the degree of your sincerity.*

5. Paraphrase what you hear people saying to you. *You might say, "Let me make sure I understand you. Your concern is . . . Is that correct?"*

6. Avoid snap judgments. *Keep your mind open until you have all the facts and thoroughly understand people's positions.*

It seems to me that as our society and business climate escalate in sophistication and complexity—with more competition and product parity—people's social and psychological needs become stronger motivators. Often, it's just the service that you give people that differentiates you from your competitors. People can probably buy what your organization sells from several other companies, but the other firms don't have you.

Daniel Goleman, in his excellent book *Primal Leadership*, writes, "First, rudeness is contagious, creating dissatisfaction, even angry customers—quite apart from whether or not a particular service matter was handled well."

He goes on: "Second, grumpy workers serve customers poorly, with sometimes devastating results: cardiac care units where nurses' general mood was 'depressed' had a death rate among patients four times higher than comparable units."

Goleman then points out, "Moreover, when service people feel upbeat, they do more to please customers: In a study of thirty-two stores in a U.S. retail chain, outlets with positive salespeople showed the best sales results."

Values such as common courtesy, friendliness, appreciation, approval, and being made to feel welcome do positively influence human relations. Customer satisfaction will move up the scale to customer loyalty to the extent that these values are given.

How you choose to practice these behaviors will determine much of your success with people.

But . . . there's still a vital emotional foundation to this.

I Can't Value You If I Don't Value Me

We come to a profound truth: *My ability to demonstrate value to others is largely dependent on the degree to which I value myself.*

William James stated an eternal truth when he wrote, "Faith creates its own verification."

My own *beliefs* about people and my ability to communicate positively with them often predict the actual event. Do I see the world, and people, in a positive or negative light? Do I think people are out to get me or that they're out looking for someone like me to help them?

Many years ago I discovered that people's service performance was usually consistent with the degree to which they valued themselves. And the degree to which they valued themselves was consistent with the level of value they perceived they created for other people. In other words: *I can like you only when I like me; I can only like me to the degree to which I see myself creating value for you.* These are the two sides of the coin.

For the last twenty-five years, my firm, Integrity Systems, has focused on helping sales and service people serve their internal and external customers most effectively. Some of the first questions we want answered as we work with people are these: *How sold are they on what they're selling? What value do they place on what they do?*

We want to know, To what extent do people believe they give customers more and better value than what they've paid for? We find that in the hustle and bustle of life, people tend to focus more on their work processes than on the value they create for internal or external customers. Or many still hold to the poverty-conscious belief, *Give me the most pay for the least work!*

We keep asking questions like these:

1. *What do you give customers that they can't get elsewhere?*
2. *What extra value do you give people above what they pay you for?*
3. *Exactly what rewards or benefits do people enjoy because of how you serve them?*

Recently, a mutual fund client told us that as a result of our training the company received $352 back for every $1 it invested with us. Alex Perriello, the president of Coldwell Banker Real Estate Corporation, told us that our "Integrity Coaching" program helped selected brokers increase their mortgage leads by 43 percent. This ran into the hundreds of millions in new business. How do you think we felt about this? How did they feel? What did this do for our relationship?

Again, let's make the point in a positive way: *I value me to the extent that I give value to you.*

This is a paradox—a seeming contradiction. But it's an emotional and spiritual truth. Unfortunately, our own natural ego, our self-focus, our "what's-in-it-for-me?" attitudes get in the way of our practicing this truth. Because of self-blindedness, many people never discover the personal power they could have otherwise enjoyed.

Often our one-sided mentality actually blocks us from enjoying the rewards of enduring success that we desperately seek.

What Value Do You Give People?

To increase your own awareness, and ultimately your success, please take some time out and ask yourself the following questions.

1. *To what extent do I value giving value to other people?*
2. *How do I give extra value to them in*
   a. *A customer service role?*
   b. *An internal service role?*
   c. *A relationship role?*
   d. *A parent role?*
   e. *A peer employee role?*
3. *How does the value I give others influence their*
   a. *Lives as customers?*
   b. *Self-esteem as people?*
   c. *View of me?*

Answering and taking action on these questions can completely change your life focus. Once you believe that you're in your current life role to create value for other people, a transformation occurs. You now see yourself in a different light. You immediately feel more valuable, confident, and vital. You work and carry yourself with more dignity and self-respect. You expect people to respect you as a person who enhances their lives.

This is a great paradox that's hidden from most people, because they don't know where and how to discover it.

In his timeless works *Think and Grow Rich* and *The Master Key to Riches*, Napoleon Hill wrote the following: "An important principle of success in all walks of life and in all occupations is a willingness to *Go the Extra Mile*; which means the rendering of more and better service than that for which one is paid, and giving it with a *positive mental attitude*."

He goes on to emphasize this seemingly contradictory principle by writing, "Man may disregard the principle if he chooses, but he cannot do so and at the same time enjoy the fruits of enduring success."

This practice of going the extra mile, according to Hill, "Keeps us on good terms with our own conscience and serves as a stimulant to our soul."

There Is Always a Compensation for This Habit

In his essay "Compensation," Emerson wrote, "Every act rewards itself, or in other words integrates itself, in a twofold manner; first in the thing, or in real nature; and second in the circumstance, or in the apparent nature."

He makes the point that the act is inseparable from the result of the act. Going on, he writes, "Cause and effect, means and ends, seeds and fruit, cannot be severed; for the effect already blooms in the cause, the end pre-exists in the means, the fruit in the seed."

Wisdom is understanding that the results of our chosen behaviors are predetermined in our choice to do these behaviors. You want to get a smile back, give one out. You want a positive response, give one out. You want respect, give it out. You want to be valued by others, value them first.

Each day you'll have numerous chances to ensure your encounters with people are positive. You'll do so by the choices you make that drive your behaviors.

What Responses Do You Want from People?

The question "What responses do you want from people?" can help you determine how to treat people in your everyday interactions—if you remember, of course, that you'll usually get back from them the attitudes and behaviors you choose to give them.

Most of us desire respect, appreciation, and recognition from people. We want them to see us "carrying our load," contributing to teamwork, making their lives easier.

Take a few moments this week. Sit down and write the positive responses you want to receive from people with whom you come in contact. Be specific about how you want certain people to respond to you. Once you've identified these desired responses, say to yourself, "Okay, if these are responses I want to receive from other people, I can best achieve them by giving the same responses to them."

Then take action and communicate this value to specific people.

You'll elevate yourself into a whole new level of communication, respect, and confidence.

The Values of Your Organization

My mother's oft-given advice was "Evil companions corrupt good morals." Or, more colloquial, "Run with goats, you'll smell like goats."

On a more sophisticated level is the term "group think." *Group think* is a phenomenon that occurs when several people are involved in a cohesive team, group, or organization. The members tend to adopt a common way of thinking, acting, and making decisions. When their collective desire for unanimity overrides each person's motivation to act according to his or her own values, deterioration can occur.

Often when *group think* occurs, the morality of a group decision can go unquestioned by the individuals within the group, as with mob psychology.

Look at some of the recent corporate scandals, where top-echelon officers seemingly forgot that the money belonged to their company and wasn't theirs to use as they personally desired. Apparently, many of their breaches were considered acceptable practices by their corporate officer peers. I suspect that most would have vehemently denied that they were crooks. Bernie Ebbers, the head of WorldCom, was also a Sunday school teacher in his church.

Often, because of the size of the organization, the responsibility for such violations becomes so diffused that it's hard to pin the blame on any single person. In time this situation can insidiously define the culture and actual value system of leaders.

Many corporate decisions are made in the context of group organizational pressures. Where does this leave the individual whose life is committed to strong ethics and values? Often this problem can bring a person to a choice of stay and conform, or find a place whose values are a match.

This quandary isn't conducive to restful nights, especially when it's the corporate leaders' values that are being compromised.

Jim Collins, in his bestselling book *Good to Great*, makes the point that every good-to-great company needs Level 5 leadership during its transition years. He explains that Level 5 leaders embody paradoxical guidelines such as personal humility and professional will. They are ambitious for their companies, not themselves. They display a compelling modesty and are self-effacing and understated. They are "more plow horses than race horses."

Collins goes on to point out that two-thirds of others profiled against good-to-great leaders had gargantuan personal egos that actually contributed to the mediocrity or demise of their organizations.

I give this brief sketch of reality to make a simple point: The self-actualized person is true to his or her values and beliefs of right and wrong, and has a life philosophy that good will prevail and that long-term success is achieved by ethical choices and actions.

These values can sometimes present hard choices, but remember—it's your life. Your sense of worth and your self-respect are some of your greatest assets. These are enhanced, or dissipated, by the moral and ethical choices you make—on and off the job.

HOW TO GAIN THE MOST FROM THIS CHAPTER

Read this chapter again with a highlighter or a pen, marking important points and making action notes for yourself.

Prepare your mind with these values:

1. *Think "You're the customer—you pay my salary!"*
2. *Think "There's something about you I like!"*
3. *Think "You make my job possible!"*

Say these sentences silently as you work with different people. Let these values guide your actions, attitudes, and behaviors this week.

When you contact people, honor them with these simple responses.

1. *Give a sincere smile.*
2. *Get people talking and you listening.*
3. *Nod as you understand and approve of what people are saying.*
4. *Verbalize your understanding of them and their needs.*
5. *Paraphrase what you hear people say to you.*
6. *Avoid snap judgments.*

Remember, regardless of who your "customers" are—internal associates, external customers, friends, spouses, family—one of their greatest needs is to be valued. When you serve up satisfaction to their needs, they'll be instinctively impelled to return this value back to you.

Take these actions, and just as the law of compensation is unerring, you'll enjoy increased rewards of respect, trust, and self-confidence.

Self-Assessment: *Value Customers*

Take a moment to read each of the following statements. Then circle the number that best describes your actions or thoughts, with *1* being "Never" and *10* being "Always."

1. The purpose of my job is to serve internal or external customers.

   1   2   3   4   5   6   7   8   9   10

2. I choose how I'll act and respond to people.

   1   2   3   4   5   6   7   8   9   10

3. I do not allow other people to determine my responses.

   1   2   3   4   5   6   7   8   9   10

4. I honor each person with whom I interact with dignity and respect.

   1   2   3   4   5   6   7   8   9   10

5. I always look for ways to give extra value to people.

   1   2   3   4   5   6   7   8   9   10

6. I try to learn from everyone I meet.

   1   2   3   4   5   6   7   8   9   10

7. I believe that serving others helps me grow stronger.

   1   2   3   4   5   6   7   8   9   10

8. I believe that all my choices plant the seeds for specific results.

   1   2   3   4   5   6   7   8   9   10

9. I choose people with whom to associate who have strong, positive values.

   1   2   3   4   5   6   7   8   9   10

10. I take complete responsibility for my daily outcomes with people.

    1   2   3   4   5   6   7   8   9   10

Action Guide: *Daily Success Diary* ✐ ✎

Value Customers

Please score yourself from 1 to 10 for each daily activity, with *1* being "Never" and *10* being "Always."

	S	M	T	W	T	F	S
1. I gave a sincere smile to each person.							
2. I got people talking and me listening.							
3. I nodded approval and understood each person.							
4. I paraphrased back to people my understanding.							
5. I avoided snap judgments.							
Total each day							

A problem well stated is a problem half solved. (Charles F. Kettering)

5 Solve Problems

Increase Your Success by
Solving Larger Problems

Many years ago a very wise man gave me some advice. I'm sure I wasn't mature enough then to comprehend its profound nature. He said, "You'll always be paid consistently with the size of problems you solve. Solve small problems and you'll receive small pay, but solve big problems and you'll enjoy big pay."

The longer I live, the more wisdom I see in his advice.

I've reflected upon it many times. I've observed other people and attempted to match this principle to their level of success. I've noticed that few people are willing to step up to the plate and take responsibility for seeing problems through to resolutions.

In a real sense, each of us controls our success level by the problems we choose to solve.

My friend and business partner, John Teets, ultimately became chairman and CEO of the Dial Corporation. In the process he earned millions of dollars. Coming from a blue-collar family, he learned early to take responsibility for results. From working in a restaurant as a dishwasher while in his teens, he was soon managing the restaurant. Then step by step he took on larger challenges.

When he's asked the secret of his incredible success, he'll tell you that he has the ability to solve problems. "I have the ability to look at complex problems and see simple solutions," he explains. "The larger the problems I took responsibility for solving, the more rewards I enjoyed."

This is true for most of us.

What Is a Problem?

A problem is the difference between what should have happened and what actually took place, as the following diagram suggests.

Usually, the size of the gap between what should have happened and what actually happened will determine the impact of the problem, as well as the rewards enjoyed when it's solved.

Problem solving isn't just in knowing how. Most of your success has to do with how you handle your emotions while in the midst of your problems. Problems elicit many emotions—fear,

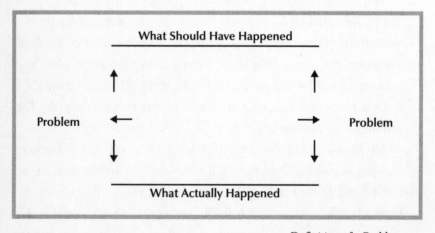

Definition of a Problem

avoidance, excitement, anticipation, and others. Emotional control is essential for problem resolution.

Problems Create Emotions

Often, emotions are involved when customers have problems. These may be their emotions, or yours, or both. When difficulties or misunderstandings do arise, a whole range of emotions can be triggered.

EMOTIONS TRIGGERED

Customer's:	*Yours:*
Anger	Defensiveness
Confusion	Denial
Irrational responses	Ego Involvement
Overly demanding attitude	Frustration

Many other emotions can be triggered, depending on the size of the problem from your customer's perspective. There is a moment of truth, a defining moment when you first discuss problems with your internal or external customers. Your attitude, tone of voice, and sincere desire to understand their thinking—all these factors create certain emotions within customers.

Your first objective is to be as calm and rational as possible, to apologize to your customers for whatever inconvenience they experienced, and to assure them that you want to make them happy. It's critical at this point that you control your own emotions and responses. When people are upset and vent emotions, it's easy to return the same emotional response to them as they give you.

Again, I refer to the law of psychological reciprocity: *People are instinctively impelled to return the same feelings and attitudes to us as we give them.*

This works both ways. When customers vent anger toward us,

it's natural to return that same level of emotion to them. But when we control our reactions, we then often help angry customers tone down their responses to us.

So, when encountering customer problems or complaints, take a deep breath and give this three-part response:

- *"On behalf of our organization, I apologize for the problem this has created."*
- *"Please help me understand what happened and what should have happened, and let's resolve this problem."*
- *"We want you to be happy."*

Usually, when you say this and sincerely mean it, you'll immediately see a softened emotional response from customers.

A Problem-Solving Formula

Here's a step-by-step formula that you can use as a problem-solving guide:

1. Understand *the problem*.
2. Identify *the cause*.
3. Discuss *possible solutions*.
4. Solve *the problem*.

I'll also share specific Action Guides for each step.

While this formula is primarily designed for customer-related problems, you'll find many other applications for it.

Ed Weber, general manager of production at Robertson Brothers Community Builders in Bloomfield Hills, Michigan, writes this about how he used the problem-solving formula:

> I always dreaded dealing with customer complaints. Now I look forward to the opportunity to solve customers' issues. In my position in the company, customers have been dissatisfied with the solutions to their problems after dealing with at least

two other levels of management by the time they call me. Using the problem-solving formula, I am able to understand, identify, discuss, and solve the problem.

Listening to my customers has been a real awakening for me. In the past, I worked to solve problems without finding out what my customer wanted. I'm now able to better serve my customers' needs by letting them tell me what they think the desired outcome should be so we can then negotiate a solution. I am spending less of my company's resources, and making my customers happy by using the problem-solving formula.

Way to go, Ed!

Step 1: Understand the Problem

Here are three Action Guides to practice to help you understand people's problems.

1. *Get all the facts.*
2. *Listen nondefensively.*
3. *Repeat back the problem as understood.*

GET ALL THE FACTS

You begin getting all the facts by saying, "Please explain to me your understanding of what happened."

Since, from your customer's perspective, a problem exists, you want to completely understand what they think and feel.

It's here that your sincere desire to get all the facts will set the stage for communication success. People intuitively know when you sincerely want to understand them, their opinions, and their concerns. When you don't show your desire to understand them, trust is often destroyed.

Not long ago I had a significant problem—at least I was told I had one. I had gone to a local clinic for an executive physical. My initial blood work showed what the doctor called a "high 'cocci' count." She explained coccidioidomycosis, a condition found in the deserts of Arizona and California. The disease, commonly called "valley fever," is a fungus that can cause respiratory difficulties, fever, and skin eruptions.

The physician sent me to a pulmonary doctor in the clinic. He did more tests and told me the problem wasn't cocci, but probably a malignancy in my left lung. I referred him back to the original blood work that showed high cocci. He said it was wrong.

He then ran all kinds of expensive tests—CAT scan, PET scan, bronchoscopy, and X-ray. Finally, he recommended surgery.

That'll get your attention.

Stupid me, I never thought about getting a second opinion. So, they cut a hole in my back about eight inches long, separated muscles, pried my ribs apart, and took out the lower lobe of my left lung.

When they did a tissue analysis, they found that it wasn't a malignancy, but guess what? Valley fever.

It was a very invasive surgery, I couldn't work at all for weeks, and then only a couple of hours a day for six months. It cost me a great deal of money in lost productivity. The only response from the doctor who made the diagnosis was "Congratulations, you've just won the lottery!" That was in a thirty-second phone call. Later, he refused to return my calls. I then found out from a researcher on valley fever at the University of Arizona that the doctor could have diagnosed the real problem by doing a simple needle biopsy.

Will I ever go back to that clinic? Probably not! Would I have ever gone back if this doctor had talked to me, answered my questions, and shown concern for my problem? Yes!

LISTEN NONDEFENSIVELY

After the bills came for this surgery, and I found that I owed around $20,000 above what my insurance would pay, I asked the clinic people why I had to pay so much for their very expensive procedures, which were wrong. They tuned me out as if I were a gnat that had splattered their windshield.

No discussion, no compromise, no real show of concern.

To show indifference for people's problems can cause walls to go up. The moment a relationship becomes stressed, a no-win situation can result.

Think back to when you had a problem with a purchase or a relationship. Remember how emotionally vulnerable you were, and how quickly you could become more negative? Or when people really cared about your satisfaction, how all of a sudden you felt your anger or frustration disappear? These are very fragile moments when relationships can be broken or strengthened. Many customers are lost this way. When they see you either blame them or dish anger back to them, things can go bad.

Listening nondefensively is being open, being calm, and wanting to know everything you can about the situation. Often, when you genuinely attempt to understand your customers' positions, you trigger like responses from them. They're then more apt to want to understand the situation from your side.

Asking questions and listening is a great way to defuse people's negative emotions. When you ask questions and listen with a calm, sincere desire to understand the answers, people will often change. Remember, it takes two to do battle.

A great question to ask is "So that I can understand your concern, would you please explain to me what has happened?"

Then listen.

Often, if you get people explaining their problem twice, they'll talk out their negative feelings. It's good to ask, after hearing their concern, "To make sure that I completely understand you, would you mind explaining that again?"

Then listen.

REPEAT BACK THE PROBLEM AS UNDERSTOOD

When you ask for clarification, or for customers to repeat the problem so you can understand it more clearly, you show that you're on their side, that solving their problem is a partnership between both sides. This gets you working together to find the best way to solve their problem.

I remember reading that Abraham Lincoln never lost a court case. It was said that at first he'd argue his opponent's case to juries. He'd tell the good points of the other side. Then, at some point, he'd say, "But let's see if there are other facts that we should consider."

Then he'd bring in his own points. He built trust with juries and then carried them with him because of his attempt at "fairness." He seemed to be on their side, helping them examine the facts.

When you truly want to understand your customers' concerns, you'll find the right questions and responses.

Step 2: Identify the Cause

Every problem has a specific cause. There's a reason that the problem occurred. Something made it happen. Once you understand the problem from your customers' perspective and let them know of your sincere desire to help them with a solution, you can proceed to identify the cause.

Often, successful problem resolution happens by *identifying* and *removing* the cause. In order to identify the cause of problems, you can practice these Action Guides. Ask these questions:

1. *"What happened?"*
2. *"What should have happened?"*
3. *"What went wrong?"*

You can introduce your fact-finding activity by saying something like this: "Again, I appreciate your contacting me about this problem. I'm sorry it happened, but since it did let's get it solved. Let me ask you some questions so I can understand what has caused this problem . . ."

Asking and getting answers to your questions can help you get to the root of the problem. When you do this in a sincere, nonaggressive manner, you'll impress people with your professionalism. You'll often help save valuable customers.

Step 3: Discuss Possible Solutions

After you've identified the cause of a problem, the next step is to find out what it will take to solve it.

Customers will help you solve many of your problems if you only ask for their help. When you get people involved in helping you find the best solution, they often surprise you with what will satisfy them. This creates an atmosphere of partnership, which can keep the situation from becoming adversarial.

"What are some possible solutions?" you might ask. Then listen. *Asking* is much more effective than *telling* them what you think is the best solution. You'll resolve conflicts much faster and keep your customers happier when you seek out options and then help them select the best one. Telling or imposing your solutions on people can intensify their negative responses. Allowing them to tell you helps bring you together.

I'll never forget a story told to me about a Chevrolet customer. I had designed a trade assistance or replacement process for Chevrolet to help resolve customer complaints. In the course of working with the staff, I heard a story about a man they called "the General."

The General was a retired high-ranking military officer who owned a Chevy Blazer. After experiencing several problems and, in his opinion, not getting satisfaction from the dealer, he began to flood huge numbers of people at Chevrolet with letters. He rattled sabers from the top to the bottom of the organization—threatening lawsuits and anything else he could think of. He quickly gained fame among Chevrolet people—like a skunk in a perfume shop.

Finally, a Chevrolet Zone employee called and talked to him in a very mild tone that got through the General's abrasiveness and anger. The employee first apologized and then listened quietly while the old soldier expressed his feelings for the umpteenth time. Apparently, he felt that no one had ever really listened to him. Everyone had responded to him with the same degree of irritation that he had brought to them, which of course only made things worse, because you don't do that to a general. But this time when he vented his wrath, a wise person patiently listened.

Finally, after the General had expelled much of his anger, the Zone person apologized again. He then explained that one option would be to trade in his truck for a new one and pay for the miles he'd put on the current Blazer.

"Oh, no!" the General responded. "I like this one. I want to keep it."

As it turned out, he didn't want a trade. He loved the truck he had and, despite the problem, wanted to keep it. All he really wanted was for someone to listen to him, take him seriously, and offer him some options. He didn't want to exercise any of the options, because that wasn't the real issue. He just wanted to be the General and to be heard, listened to, and valued. He wasn't accustomed to being tuned out.

The General loved the nice branch person who had listened to him and began to write letters to Chevrolet executives praising the employee.

Interesting lesson, isn't it?

When you discuss possible solutions, these actions will help you:

1. *Ask for customers' ideas.*
2. *Suggest options.*
3. *Agree on the best course of action.*

Chevrolet learned that if you give people more options, they make happier customers. In this case, the extra option was to trade in the old car for a new one and receive a more-than-fair price for the used vehicle. This not only showed Chevrolet's sensitivity to customers' concerns, it also allowed the customers to focus on the positive resolution rather than on the conflict.

The General's responses were a great example of human action and reaction. When someone listened to him and offered him a new solution, his anger was neutralized, because he no longer felt pushed around.

Psychologically speaking, when we ask for customers' ideas about the best course of action, we usually cause them to become more lenient and forgiving. It helps them soften the position that they had felt forced to defend. When you take away your own resistance, it makes it all right for the customer to compromise.

The question "What do you feel is the best solution?" often causes disgruntled people to become much more pliable and eager to work with you. It causes them to refocus from negative to positive.

Does this always work? No! Because customers aren't always right, or even fair, but those who would take unfair advantage of you are usually in a minority.

Often, your wanting to know causes both you and your customer to feel that you're on the same side, with the same objective of achieving a win-win solution.

Step 4: Solve the Problem

Here are three Action Guides for solving the problem.

1. *Remove the cause.*
2. *Take corrective action.*
3. *Ask if the customer is satisfied with the resolution.*

When you and the customer have agreed on the best course of action, it's time to take that action. If the corrective action is one the customer suggested or agreed to, you have won that person's respect and loyalty.

It's here that your sincere desire to help people can be demonstrated by your actions. When people see that you want to help them, and aren't just trying to manipulate them into your own rigid solutions, your trust and rapport will be strengthened. This gives you a terrific opportunity to cement relationships with them that will cause them to want to continue to do business with you.

There are two times you can ask if your customer is satisfied with the resolution. The first is when both of you have agreed on the appropriate outcome, and you ask if that resolution will satisfy them. The second is later, when you've followed up to see if everything is satisfactory.

Dr. Art Mollen is a well-known fixture here in Phoenix. He has a sincere warmth about him that shows he loves being a doctor and helping people. He often follows up to make sure his patients are doing all right. Time after time he has called me after a visit to his offices to explain a test result or just to see how I was feeling. This level of concern and courtesy isn't exactly common, but doesn't it stick out when it occurs?

Great Customer Service Is an Attitude, Not a Strategy

The problem-solving formula I have shared with you is only a set of guidelines. The degree to which they work is determined by your own attitude, values, and emotional responses.

Successful outcomes that lead to customer loyalty result from a convergence of knowledge, motives, values, willingness to act, and having a customer focus. Notice the "Problem-Solving Convergence Model" shown below.

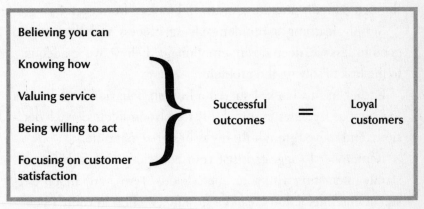

Problem-Solving Convergence Model

Leni Patton, Gift Shop manager on board the SS *Norway*, reported the following results from our "The Customer" program: "What seemed to help me the most was the problem-solving formula. When applied, passengers appeared happier with the outcome. Before your course, when a dissatisfied passenger came to me, my attitude was 'Here we go again!' Now problems are fun because I know they will be solved positively. I have the awareness and control to change situations into the right perspective."

Yes, great customer service is an attitude, not just a strategy.

Our Self-Beliefs Determine the
Size of Problems We'll Attempt to Solve

Now we come to a most important issue: Our own self-image will usually determine the size of problems we'll attempt to solve. When we see a problem as being bigger than our capacity to solve it, we'll usually avoid it, or not even consider the possibility that we could handle it.

Each of us has a well-formed internal view of our capabilities, our possibilities, and the level of problems we think we can solve. This unconscious belief is so powerful that either it will guide us through difficult situations, or it will block us from even trying.

Simply learning a problem-solving process will do us little good unless we, deep down, emotionally, believe we're adequate to the task of solving the problem.

Earlier in this book, I shared a human behavior model. Let's look at it as it relates to our ability to solve problems, make decisions, and move through thorny issues. (See opposite.)

Remember I suggested that your conscious "I Think" is constantly interacting with your unconscious "I Am," and that the result of that interaction creates a specific emotion in your "I Feel." Let's look at some of these interactions and the emotions that are triggered.

For example: If you *intellectually* ("I Think") know how to solve problems, but you *unconsciously* ("I Am") believe you cannot, that interaction will trigger *emotions* ("I Feel") of lack of confidence or avoidance. On the other hand, if you don't *unconsciously*, in your "I Am," believe you can handle problems or decisions of a certain size, the conflicting emotions in your "I Feel" will cause your "I Think" to shut down and you'll not take any kind of action. Or you may attempt to solve a problem, but if deep within your "I Am" you don't feel worthy of higher success, you'll unconsciously find a way to retreat and avoid going further.

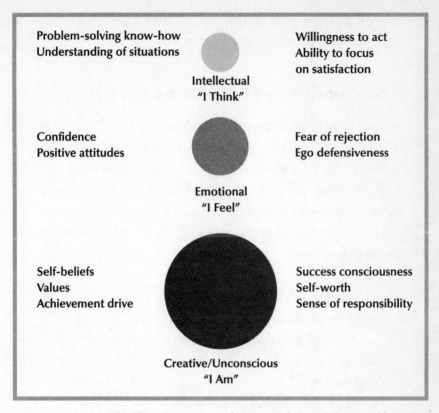

Problem-solving know-how
Understanding of situations

Intellectual
"I Think"

Willingness to act
Ability to focus
on satisfaction

Confidence
Positive attitudes

Emotional
"I Feel"

Fear of rejection
Ego defensiveness

Self-beliefs
Values
Achievement drive

Creative/Unconscious
"I Am"

Success consciousness
Self-worth
Sense of responsibility

The Three Dimensions of Human Behavior: Solving Problems

Your individual self-beliefs, values, achievement drive, success consciousness, feelings of worthiness, and sense of responsibility will all determine what size problems you're willing to tackle and solve.

So it's important to know how to solve problems, but your actual outcomes will be shaped more by your unconscious beliefs about your abilities than by your actual knowledge of how-to.

This is why so much of this book is designed to help you with your own personal growth. Knowledge alone has little or no impact upon our inner beliefs about our possibilities or worthiness. These are developed only in the stream of everyday life as you apply the actions that I'll give you in this chapter. Successful experiences breed successful expectations.

Your Behavior Style Will Influence Your Outcomes

Your individual behavior style, shown in the "Behavior Styles Model" in Chapter 2, will also influence your ability to solve problems. Your style can cause you to meet them head-on or try to duck them; you may be quick to take action, or slower and more analytical in your approach.

Here are a few ideas about how different styles might react to problem solving.

DOERS
- *Welcome problems.*
- *Make quick decisions.*
- *May rush past customers and try to impose their will.*
- *Will have trouble listening enough.*

CONTROLLERS
- *Will be very logical and efficient.*
- *Are facts-oriented.*
- *May be too cool and aloof.*
- *May not understand or deal with customers' emotional concerns.*

SUPPORTERS
- *Have high concern for customers' feelings.*
- *May not be assertive enough.*
- *Will play by the rules.*
- *Need guidance in resolutions.*

TALKERS
- *Avoid problems.*
- *Look for popular solutions.*
- *Need help from others.*
- *Easily reverse decisions.*

Remember that you're probably a combination of two styles, maybe three. How do you see yourself in these descriptors?

On the flip side, let's think about your customers' styles, and how you can identify and react to them.

WITH *DOERS*, YOU SHOULD BEHAVE LIKE THIS:

- *Expect strong opinions.*
- *Draw them out; don't argue.*
- *Ask them to give you their idea of best solutions.*
- *Expect quick responses.*

WITH *CONTROLLERS*, YOU SHOULD BEHAVE LIKE THIS:

- *Ask for specifics about what happened.*
- *Expect some criticism of you or your organization.*
- *Ask how to remedy the situation.*
- *Match their tone of voice and emotional level.*

WITH *SUPPORTERS*, YOU SHOULD BEHAVE LIKE THIS:

- *Listen carefully—they may not be specific or direct at first.*
- *Show your respect for their feelings.*
- *Suggest options clearly.*
- *Honor their need for safety and security.*

WITH *TALKERS*, YOU SHOULD BEHAVE LIKE THIS:

- *Listen and don't interrupt.*
- *Make friends with them.*
- *Ask about their family and their interests.*
- *Ask what will make them happy.*

Understanding your own style and its natural tendencies, along with recognizing your customers' styles, will help you communicate effectively with them. When you can identify and match their style, you'll gain rapport more easily. This will cause them to subconsciously feel better about you and to be more willing to work out a win-win solution.

HOW TO GAIN THE MOST FROM THIS CHAPTER

Say to yourself each day, "I get paid consistently with the size of problems I solve."

Think about the level of pay—self-respect, level of success, salary, respect from others—you'd like to enjoy. Then ask yourself, "What size problems will I need to solve in order to receive these increased rewards?"

Then, if you truly want the payoffs you've identified, take action and tackle the problems that come at you daily.

You learned this problem-solving formula:

1. Understand *the problem.*
2. Identify *the cause.*
3. Discuss *possible solutions.*
4. Solve *the problem.*

Let me emphasize that your ability to solve problems involves much more than just knowing the formula. It's really a holistic issue. You must bring these elements into convergence.

- *Believing you can*
- *Knowing how*
- *Valuing service*
- *Being willing to act*
- *Focusing on customer satisfaction*

These intellectual, emotional, and value issues all affect your ultimate ability to solve problems.

Also, it helps to understand the conscious and unconscious interplay within you as you face problems. Your conscious choices or actions will interact with your inner self-beliefs and values to produce emotions of confidence or avoidance. These resulting emotions can then either build up your confidence or shoot you down.

Try to evaluate your performance each day in the following

Daily Success Diary. Remember—*Behavior that gets measured gets improved.*

And finally . . . just about every organization in the world is looking for people who will step up to the plate and take responsibility for solving problems that enhance customer satisfaction and loyalty.

In a real sense, you can *choose* the level of success you want to enjoy by the size of the problems you *choose* to solve.

Self-Assessment: *Solve Problems*

Take a moment to read each of the following statements. Then circle the number that best describes your actions or thoughts, with *1* being "Never" and *10* being "Always."

1. I confidently face problems rather than ignore them.

   1   2   3   4   5   6   7   8   9   10

2. I view problem solving as a positive way to develop customer loyalty.

   1   2   3   4   5   6   7   8   9   10

3. People often ask me to help them solve problems.

   1   2   3   4   5   6   7   8   9   10

4. I never allow my own ego to get in the way of problem solving.

   1   2   3   4   5   6   7   8   9   10

5. I thoroughly listen to customers' concerns before forming an opinion.

   1   2   3   4   5   6   7   8   9   10

6. I never allow myself to become defensive or combative.

   1   2   3   4   5   6   7   8   9   10

7. I see problem solving as a win-win situation.

   1   2   3   4   5   6   7   8   9   10

8. I allow customers to share their thoughts as well as their feelings.

   1   2   3   4   5   6   7   8   9   10

9. I follow up to make sure the customer is satisfied with the resolution.

   1   2   3   4   5   6   7   8   9   10

10. I listen and determine customers' behavior styles and guide my responses accordingly.

   1   2   3   4   5   6   7   8   9   10

Action Guide: *Daily Success Diary*

Solve Problems

Please score yourself from 1 to 10 for each daily activity, with *1* being "Never" and *10* being "Always."

	S	M	T	W	T	F	S
1. I *understood* the problem.							
a. I got all the facts.							
b. I listened nondefensively.							
c. I repeated back the problem as understood.							
2. I *identified* the cause.							
a. "What happened?"							
b. "What should have happened?"							
c. "What went wrong?"							
3. I *discussed* possible solutions.							
a. I suggested options.							
b. I asked for customers' ideas.							
c. I agreed on the best course of action.							
4. I *solved* the problem.							
a. I removed the cause.							

(continued on next page)

	S	M	T	W	T	F	S
4. I *solved* the problem. *(continued)*							
b. I took corrective action.							
c. I asked if the customer was satisfied with the resolution.							
Total each day							

Wisdom is the principal thing; therefore get wisdom: and with all thy getting get understanding. (Proverbs 4:7)

6 Ask How to Help Customers

Find Out What Needs People Have That You Can Help Them Fill

"My associates and I get frequent calls from a man we've collectively labeled 'The Grouch.' " This was how a participant in a course I was conducting began her talk. She worked in a city tax office.

> The Grouch would frequently call and point out our mistakes, complain about valuations, and generally create havoc. Everyone in the office dreaded his calls with a high degree of mortal terror.
>
> Sure enough, it was my luck to receive his next call. In a very derisive tone, he was complaining about some tax evaluations. I let him talk and, in a couple of moments, said in a jolly, over-the-top way, "Mr. [she called his name], everyone in this office is afraid of you, but I'll bet that you're really a nice man. Why, I'll bet that your kids even like you. I'd like to meet you some time and understand your business so I can serve you better."

There was a pregnant pause. Then The Grouch just died laughing and said, "I like you. Can I call you any time I need help?"

"Of course you can," I replied.

The next day a man came into the tax office with a box of candy and asked to see her. It was The Grouch. He apologized to her; she introduced him to her associates; and everyone enjoyed the candy. After that, he received open welcomes to his calls. And he no longer deserved the nickname they'd previously given him.

What was his need? What motivated him to bring the candy? What got by his outer crustiness?

Everyone Has a Reason for Contacting You

Internal associates and external customers each have a reason for their contacts with you. They all have unique needs, wants, or problems they're looking to satisfy or solve. For the sake of semantics, we'll lump all these reasons together and use the word "needs."

Customers' needs range from the obvious ones to more emotional or ego-driven ones. Here are a few different kinds of needs people have.

- *For a specific product or service*
- *For a solution to a problem*
- *For specific rewards*
- *For personal gratification*
- *To make themselves look good to others, or to receive recognition*
- *To be viewed as a person who's responsible*
- *To feel good about themselves*
- *To get ahead on the job*
- *To be listened to and understood*
- *To form healthy relationships*

Usually customers have several needs—not just one, as did The Grouch. Ironically, I knew him. He had been a client of mine several years before I heard our course participant's story. As I listened to her talk about him, not mentioning his name, a picture of him popped into my mind. I asked her at the break, "Was that Mr. Ketler?" She responded, "Yes, how did you know that?"

Oh yes, you were introduced to him in a previous chapter of this book.

He was a small man who smoked big cigars and barked loudly. Behind his need to intimidate others, he was really a nice man who needed lots of personal recognition. He was an off-the-charts Controller. He demanded accuracy and had little patience with anyone who made the slightest mistake. Those who could get beyond his outer facade found him to have a unique sense of humor. He was extremely loyal to people he liked or trusted.

So, instead of my previous question, "What was his need?" let's now ask, "What were his *needs?*" He had several.

Most people have a combination of different needs. Usually one or two are dominant in different parts of a person's life.

Let's dig deeper.

Types of Needs People Have

Study the model below, and you'll see that our motivations usually involve several needs that we want filled.

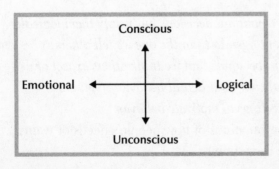

Types of Needs

Here are a few examples of each of these needs.

EMOTIONAL

- *To look good*
- *To not look bad*
- *To receive gratification*
- *To be valued, listened to, and understood*
- *To express feelings, ego, and personality*

LOGICAL

- *To solve problems*
- *To get the right products or services*
- *To receive specific, measured value*
- *To be accurate*
- *To not run risks*

These needs can drive people's buying or service decisions either consciously or unconsciously. People may know what will fill their needs, or they may have needs but be unaware of solutions. Or they may have inner drives that cause them to make decisions, not being conscious of what's really motivating them.

For instance:

CONSCIOUS

- *To understand what drives us*
- *To know what we want or need*
- *To have a clear picture of desired outcomes*
- *To clearly identify rewards sought*
- *To be able to articulate what we want or need*

UNCONSCIOUS

- *To buy or make emotional decisions but justify them logically*
- *To have a different agenda than the one we tell others*
- *To act out certain personas that we think others expect of us*
- *To act consistently with our actual behavior style*
- *To allow inner feelings to motivate behavior*

I mention these combinations of how people's needs or wants are expressed to make these points.

1. *Some people make* logical *decisions and want their communication with you to be on an objective level.*
2. *Other people make* emotional *decisions and want communication to be on a personal level.*
3. *Some people are* conscious *of what will satisfy their needs, wants, and drives.*
4. *Other people are* unconscious *of their actual needs, wants, or drives and need help in discovering a solution.*

Your job as a professional is to understand how you can help customers enjoy satisfaction. This means not only that you understand their needs and help fill them, but also that you help them with solutions they aren't aware exist.

Perhaps you quickly identify what will satisfy a person, you recommend a solution, the person accepts it, and the transaction is completed. Or the person may want to take more time to make sure it's the best solution.

You'll want to give attention to the person's natural behavior styles. Each style has different needs for touch, information, decision process, and relationship with you.

All these factors make people's buying or decision motives quite complicated; but just trying to understand them puts you ahead of most others with whom they have contact.

Ask How to Help Customers

As we think about people's needs and reasons for acting, let's move to the third step of our G. *Val Hi* customer communication process: *Ask how to help customers.*

The Action Guides for this step follow:

1. *Ask people "How may I help you?"*
2. *Find out why the person came in or contacted you.*
3. *Ask open-ended, indirect questions to further understand people's needs.*

Ask "How May I Help You?"

After you've *greeted* customers and *valued* them as important people who make your job possible, the third step is to *ask* how you might help them.

You may use different words in asking this—that will depend on the nature of your relationship or on your profession. Your sincere desire to know how you can help people will color the way you ask.

Keith DeGreen is head of a financial services organization in Phoenix. He also has a Sunday-morning radio program that I tune into while driving to church.

He has excellent communication skills, and as he takes calls, he says, "Thank you for calling in . . . How may we [he has some associates in the studio with him] help you?"

He sounds completely sincere when he says this. There's a special graciousness to his voice and attitude.

It's here that your tone of voice and the degree to which you internally value the customer are communicated both consciously and subconsciously to people. Think of your communication effectiveness as being 15 percent the words you say and 85 percent your sincerity and reason for saying them. I throw these numbers out not as a research-driven fact, but simply to emphasize the importance of your motives.

YOUR REASON FOR ASKING

It's typical for service people to ask "How may I help you?" To their credit, they may ask that so often that it loses much of its intended meaning. Hey, I've been guilty of this myself.

We've all encountered people who display two main motivations for asking how they can help us.

- *They really, sincerely, want to know,* or
- *They're routinely going through the motions of asking.*

You've experienced people who clearly fit both motives, haven't you? Take the airline ticket agent who couldn't care less about your missed connection and is just trying to get you to a cheap motel for four hours' sleep so you can catch an early-morning flight. He lets you know by his lack of eye contact that you're just a number in a long line of problem people who are ruining his evening.

Or maybe you're lucky enough to have a ticket agent like the American Airlines one I recently had in Dallas. She apologized, calling me by my name, for the lateness of my flight from New York, which missed the last connection of the day to Phoenix. She asked me if I lived in Phoenix, how long, and how I liked it. This took probably an extra minute of her time, but she connected with me. She filled my need to feel important. Her sincere attitude kept me from venting or taking out my frustration on her. I suspect that her positive attitude also kept other customers from showing their irritation.

Two types of responses—two different motives.

TESTING THE POWER OF YOUR MOTIVES

Here's an exercise you can do with another person that proves the power of your motives or attitudes when asking how you can help someone. It's an experiment in kinesiology, or the impact of thoughts and emotions upon the physical body.

You can do this by asking another person of your size and physical strength to hold up his or her strongest arm so it's horizontal with the floor. Ask the person to clinch her fist and resist your attempt to pull her arm down. Your purpose is to simply test this person's arm strength against yours. When you pull down, don't jerk or put all your weight on the person's arm. Just pull down in a steady way.

After you've tested her strength, ask her to drop her arm to a relaxed position, close her eyes, and visualize an internal or external customer whom she serves or with whom she works. Then suggest that she visualize this specific person and silently say, "I sincerely want to understand how I can help you." Ask her to repeat this silent command three or four times. Then ask her to raise her arm again and resist as much as possible as you test her arm strength again.

After doing this, thank the person and ask her to drop her arm, keep this mental picture of the same internal or external customer, and silently say, "I really don't care about you; I'm just going about my job."

After she has said this silently to herself three or four times, ask her to raise her arm and test her strength again.

You'll find that the person has lost much of of his or her strength this last time.

Then, if you're still unconvinced, have the other person do this exercise with you—where it's your arm that's being tested.

Now, let me emphasize that the magic of this is only understood as you do it. You can't understand it logically.

"What's the point of all this?" you ask. It's this: The thoughts, attitudes, or actions we choose to take cause us to be physically strong or weak. And since we're interconnected—body, mind, spirit—strength or weakness in one area influences our strength in the other areas.

Why does this work? Go back to our "Three Dimensions of Human Behavior" model. With your "I Think," you chose a particular response—positive or negative. When you consciously choose to ask how you can help people because you sincerely want to help them, that choice interacts with the internal values in your unconscious "I Am." This congruent interaction then causes your muscles to be strong.

The simple truth is that when you select appropriate actions that are congruent with positive values, you immediately trigger strong physical and emotional responses. You have no voluntary control of the actual response. Choices of honesty, sincerity, and a genuine concern for others interact with your unconscious beliefs, values, and truth to produce

- *strong muscular responses*, and
- *strong emotional responses of confidence, enthusiasm, and self-worth.*

So whenever you *greet* people, *value* them, and *ask* how you might help them, remember to take a second or two to check your motives—realizing their influence upon your physical and emotional strength.

Remember, too, that your feelings will be subliminally communicated to your customers, as well as influencing your own energy and emotions.

Find Out Why They Called or Contacted You

Why *do* customers and associates have contact with you? What needs, wants, or problems do they have that you can help them fill, satisfy, or solve? When you view the purpose of your job as a value creator, or problem solver, your focus is on people's specific needs and how you can help them.

Whether it's a problem, a solution, or just a question that causes people to come to you, once you've greeted and valued them, you want to find out how you can help them. There's a tendency, especially if you're a Doer or a Controller, to tell people about a product, service, or solution before even knowing what they want.

I walked into an electronics store one day needing to pick up some batteries for a cordless phone in my home. As I walked in, I stopped and looked at a plasma television set. Immediately, a salesperson came up and began trying to sell it to me. Never asking any questions, he droned on and on about the picture quality, and so forth.

I thought I was going to have to fake heart failure to get him off his attack mode. When I showed him the battery pack that I wanted replaced, he acted as if I'd just deprived his children and his children's children of any future hope of survival.

If he had attempted to find out why I came in and had addressed my real need, he would have gained a stronger relationship with me than he did.

As it was, I felt guilty for weeks because I'd deprived his family lineage of any future hope. His offspring will probably know only poverty and ignorance because of my refusal to buy the TV from him.

Ask Open-Ended, Indirect Questions

It was Rudyard Kipling who wrote:

I keep six honest serving men
They taught me all I knew;
Their names are What and Why and When
And How and Where and Who.

Open-ended questions are ones that contain one of these "six honest serving men."

- *Who*
- *What*
- *Where*
- *Why*
- *When*
- *How*

Using these words calls for explanations from people. Questions that call for a "yes" or "no" response are often communication stoppers. Open-ended questions get you the information you need to know so you can better understand people's needs.

Whatever situation you find yourself in with customers—whether you're in a problem-solving, retail, or service situation—you must know what people need from you. It helps to remember that people don't want your product or service for what it is; rather, they want the end-result benefit it will give them. Sound simple? Yes, it is, but go into a dozen different sales or service places and see just how many people actually practice this.

Again, open-ended questions help you understand what end-result benefits your customers want. This tells you their motive for buying.

On one occasion, I went into the Ralph Lauren Polo Store in the Biltmore Fashion Park here in Phoenix. Spyros Maduros, who has been a fixture there for well over a decade, greeted me and shook my hand in his usual friendly way. He asked about my travels, my grandsons' college experiences, and how he could help me. I told him that I needed some casual shirts and slacks. "How will you be using them?" he asked.

I told him that I was going on a cruise. "Oh, tell me where?"

"The Caribbean," I replied.

"What cruise line?"

"The new *Queen Mary 2*."

"What will the weather be?"

I told him.

"Are you going to wear the white blazer I sold you?" he asked.

"Yes. How did you remember? That was two years ago."

"I remember everything," he said with a smile.

He asked several other questions and then pulled out some shirts and slacks to show me. I picked up a shirt and asked him about it, and he said, "No, you don't want that. It won't wear well."

As usual, my shopping experience with him was very pleasurable. He never asked me what I wanted; rather, he asked me open-ended, indirect questions to determine how I would use the clothes. When he understood my intended use, he then made recommendations.

Understand and practice this process, and you'll put yourself ahead of the herd, because few sales or service people know to do this. They're usually too product- or process-focused.

The Purpose of Your Questions

Again, the reason you ask open-ended questions is to get information that helps you determine people's desired objectives. Here are a few kinds of information you may want to get with your questions.

1. *Problems they want to solve*
2. *Solutions they're seeking*
3. *Goals they want to reach*
4. *Needs they want filled*
5. *Wants they desire satisfied*
6. *Help they need from you*
7. *Answers they want*
8. *End-result benefits they want to enjoy*
9. *Gratification they desire*
10. *Treatment they want from you*

Aside from finding out exactly what people want from a transaction, you'll want to remember this maxim: *People are more apt to act upon ideas that they discover for themselves than ones we tell them.*

Said another way: People are more motivated by their own discoveries than they are by our thoughts or advice. So how can you ask people appropriate, open-ended, indirect questions that get them discovering their true needs? Spyros knew not to ask me what kind of clothes I wanted. Rather, he asked for *how* and *when* I would wear them; then he recommended the *what*.

Help People Paint Mental Pictures of Their Desired Gratification

By asking open-ended questions, with the sincere desire to understand people's wants or needs, you can often cause them to either change their thinking or discover for themselves what the best solution would be. Either way, when their real needs are discovered and admitted, you're in a position to make recommendations.

Fundamentally, we all make purchase or service decisions when we perceive the gratification or rewards will exceed the consequences of the cost of money, time, or risk. This is also true of relationships—either internal associates or external customers.

Knowing that people must believe the rewards they'll enjoy will exceed the costs they'll pay, great service providers not only help people admit or discover their wants or needs, but also help them visualize the rewards they'll enjoy.

Notice the following model, "Current versus Desired Situation Gap."

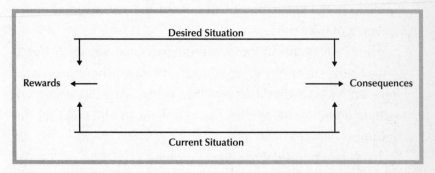

Current versus Desired Situation Gap

Before people make decisions about product or service purchases, they either consciously or unconsciously go through this thinking process.

1. *"What is my current situation?"*
2. *"What is my desired situation?"*
3. *"What are the rewards for taking action?"*
4. *"What are the consequences of taking action versus staying where I am now?"*

What thought process did you go through the last time you bought an automobile? Do any of the following thoughts seem familiar?

CURRENT SITUATION

- *My old car needs new tires.*
- *It's got too many miles on it.*
- *I could experience a major maintenance problem at any time.*
- *But at least it's paid for.*
- *I could probably drive it another year or so.*

DESIRED SITUATION

- *The new models sure look great.*
- *My brother-in-law is always showing off his new car.*
- *A new one would be great to take on our vacation.*
- *I'm kind of tired of our old one.*
- *The new models get better gas mileage.*

Well, you can fill in the blanks about the rewards and consequences of not acting.

Here's my point: In almost all interpersonal, service, or problem-solving situations there is a gap between where people are now and where they'd like to be. Where gaps do occur and people admit them, you'll often ask them to articulate the following:

- *Consequences of not taking action*
- *Rewards of acting*

Both the rewards of acting and the consequences of not taking action become motivators when people are asked to think of both. Look at the following "Motivation to Action Model."

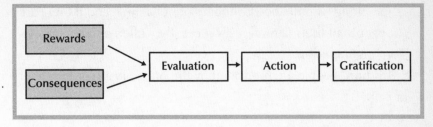

Motivation to Action Model

Here's how our minds work.

1. *We often have a natural resistance to change or to run risks. We have natural human emotions like fear of mistakes, fear of loss, fear of looking bad, fear of risk.*

2. *This resistance is overcome by focusing on the rewards we'll enjoy by making decisions or taking action—and by logically thinking of the consequences we'll suffer by not taking action or making decisions.*

3. *When we've evaluated our situation, and our hope of rewards and desire to avoid consequences are strong enough, we are motivated to take action. When we take action, we then enjoy the gratification we desire.*

Understanding these basic motivations suggests a way to help people clarify or discover needs they have. It's not a way to manipulate them, or to get them to do what we want them to do, but to help guide their thinking.

When you ask appropriate questions that get people going through these thought processes, you'll often cause them to experience powerful emotions, and this often motivates them to act.

When you ask open-ended questions in your attempt to understand people's wants or needs, you'll often help them sort through their thinking and gain a clearer understanding of what they desire to happen. Then they weigh the rewards that they might enjoy, along with the consequences of not acting, and if these are stronger than their natural resistances, they often come to a decision or conclusion.

In short, people are motivated by the hope of gain or the relief of pain.

Asking Questions and Listening Helps Strengthen Rapport

Rapport forms as you ask questions and listen to people. You can strengthen your trust when you listen without a preconceived agenda and when your own objective is to understand the person and what he or she thinks or wants to happen.

Since communication is a two-way street, as you listen to people, occasionally paraphrase to them your understanding of what they're telling you. Maybe it's an internal associate who's explaining a new policy of expense reports or purchasing processes. Your paraphrase might be "I understand how I should fill in my expense reports. It's this way. . . . Am I correct?"

Or to a customer you might respond, "If I understand your situation, you want running shoes that give you the most support. Is that correct?"

Paraphrasing is simply repeating to a person your understanding of what he or she tells you. It's a great way to connect with people and show your sincere interest in them. It draws both of you together.

People's Needs Aren't Always Logical Ones

You must always remember that we human beings are in essence *human beings*. It's my belief that on average we're 15 percent logical and 85 percent emotional in our purchasing and interactions with others. We usually have a lot going on in our minds that we don't reveal to others with our words. Often we make emotional decisions and then present them in purely logical terms. We hide our real motivations.

Everyone has different motives or reasons for taking action. Here are the four basic motives:

- *Pride*
- *Pleasure*
- *Profit*
- *Peace*

Pride impells us to look good: We want others to perceive us as important, and we want not to be proven wrong. Doers and Talkers will be more motivated by pride than Controllers and Supporters are. Pride often emanates from our egos. We want to win and not lose—to be proven right, not to be made to look bad.

Talkers' pride motivation is usually expressed in their need to be liked or receive social approval. They want you to perceive them as your friends. They're also *pleasure* motivated—to enjoy, to have a good time.

Doers exhibit pride in a totally different way. They want you to respect, admire, and look up to them for their status, achievements, or success level. Your respecting them is more important to them than your liking them. They want you to defer to them because of your respect for who they are. They don't like to be interrupted or for you to assume you know more than they do.

Controllers' dominant motive is often *profit*. Since they're logical, unemotional people, they'll want logical, unemotional results. Usually their desired results are to get a good deal, to save, or to be efficient. They're not swayed by flashy things that call attention to themselves. In fact, they'll usually avoid such things. Also, be careful to match their voice tone and emotional level.

Supporters' main motivation is *peace*—peace of mind, avoidance of undue risks, insurance from future loss. They're inclined to stay with the tried-and-true. They're more interested in safety and security than the more positive benefits of enjoyment or gratification. They're not out to call attention to themselves, as are Talkers and Doers.

When you carefully observe people's actions, tone of voice, dress, and mannerisms, you can begin to understand their behavioral style. As you begin to notice certain telltale signs, and change your style to match theirs, you'll communicate more successfully with customers. You'll also begin to address deeper needs they have.

To prepare your mind to understand people's needs, wants, problems, or desired solutions, adopt these beliefs or values:

1. *"I want to understand you."*
2. *"I want to understand what you want."*
3. *"I want to understand the rewards you want to enjoy."*
4. *"I want to understand your behavior style so I can communicate most effectively with you."*
5. *"I want to know what will make you happy."*

Also, learn the power of asking questions. Put aside your own need to tell or dominate the talking, and ask questions that draw out people's opinions and thoughts. When your objective is to understand customers' needs, wants, or problems, the more skilled you are at asking questions, the more successful you'll become.

HOW TO GAIN THE MOST FROM THIS CHAPTER

In this chapter we've shown that everyone with whom you have contact has specific needs, wants, problems, or desired solutions. To find out what they are, you ask questions. You practice the following Action Guides.

1. *Ask people "How may I help you?"*
2. *Find out why the person came in or contacted you.*
3. *Ask open-ended, indirect questions to further understand people's needs.*

I've emphasized that you should ask questions because you really, sincerely want to know how you can help people.

I've suggested a simple kinesthetic experiment that dramatically shows the impact of your thoughts, attitudes, and motives upon your physical and emotional strength. Try it out on several people, and see what you learn by doing it.

We've thought about the "six honest serving men" that Kipling wrote about: *who, what, where, why, when, how.* These create open-ended questions that call for explanations and get customers or associates talking and you listening.

Your objective with questions is not only to understand people's needs or wants but also to get people to express them so *they* discover and understand them more clearly. Remember this principle: *People are more apt to act upon ideas that they discover for themselves than ones we tell them.* Following this truth underscores the importance of your questions.

As you go about understanding individuals' needs, make every effort to understand and match their behavior styles. This will help you get clarity on their underlying needs or wants.

You can prepare your mind for greater success with people by repeating these self-suggestions again and again.

1. *"I want to understand you."*
2. *"I want to understand what you want."*
3. *"I want to understand the rewards you want to enjoy."*
4. *"I want to understand your behavior style so I can communicate most effectively with you."*
5. *"I want to know what will make you happy."*

It may sound mechanical, but actually repeating these statements to yourself over and over will in time program them into your mind as values and self-beliefs. This really works. The deeper the programming, the more these strong, positive responses will be exhibited in your unconscious behaviors.

And . . . both you and your customer will enjoy an increased sense of value.

Self-Assessment: *Ask How to Help Customers*

Take a moment to read each of the following statements. Then circle the number that best describes your actions or thoughts, with *1* being "Never" and *10* being "Always."

1. I focus on customers' needs for value, rather than on my own needs.

   1   2   3   4   5   6   7   8   9   10

2. I sincerely want to understand how to help people.

   1   2   3   4   5   6   7   8   9   10

3. I never present solutions to people until I understand their needs or wants.

   1   2   3   4   5   6   7   8   9   10

4. I make every effort to focus on each customer or internal associate whom I serve.

   1   2   3   4   5   6   7   8   9   10

5. I send positive thoughts to the people with whom I communicate.

   1   2   3   4   5   6   7   8   9   10

6. I am very good at asking open-ended questions.

   1   2   3   4   5   6   7   8   9   10

7. I always attempt to understand a person's behavior style in the questions I ask.

   1   2   3   4   5   6   7   8   9   10

8. I am very good at determining what people want from my transactions.

   1   2   3   4   5   6   7   8   9   10

9. I am constantly improving my skill of understanding people's dominant motives.

   1   2   3   4   5   6   7   8   9   10

10. I often receive thanks from customers and internal associates for my sincere interest in them.

    1   2   3   4   5   6   7   8   9   10

Action Guide: *Daily Success Diary* ✐ ✎

Ask How to Help Customers

Please score yourself from 1 to 10 for each daily activity, with *1* being "Never" and *10* being "Always."

	S	M	T	W	T	F	S
1. I asked, "How may I help you?"							
2. I found out why people came in or contacted me.							
3. I asked open-ended questions to further understand people's needs.							
4. I said to myself several times each day, "I really want to know how I can help you."							
5. I identified each person's behavior style.							
Total each day							

The price of greatness is responsibility. (Winston Churchill)

7 Assume Responsibility

Make and Keep Commitments
That Get Results

Around the turn of the twentieth century, a little book was published because of a sudden whim of the author, and it was soon printed in every language in the world, selling hundreds of millions of copies. Corporate executives gave it to all their employees; governments gave it to everyone in their armies; individuals bought it from shelves and catalogs in an unprecedented way. Perhaps no book, outside the Bible, had ever sold as many copies as this book did.

A *Message to Garcia* was penned by Elbert Hubbard in a moment of inspiration. It brought a simple message to anyone who sought success, personal stewardship, and effectiveness— *individual responsibility.*

The story began when President Theodore Roosevelt called a general into his office during the Spanish-American War and told him he wanted a message delivered to a man named Garcia somewhere in the hills of Cuba, where the war was being fought. The general knew just the man to do the job—a man named

Rowan. "If anyone can take the message to Garcia, Rowan can," was the general's assertion.

So he summoned Rowan and handed him a pouch with this simple order: "Take this letter to a man named Garcia who is fighting a battle somewhere in the hills of Cuba."

Rowan took the letter, saluted, and turned to go to find a man named Garcia who was fighting a battle in the hills of Cuba.

Hubbard told the story and made these points:

- *Rowan did not ask, "Where in Cuba is Garcia?"*
- *He did not ask, "How will I know him when I find him?"*
- *He did not ask, "What is in the letter?"*
- *He did not ask any questions. He simply took the letter and said, "Yes, sir," saluted, and turned to go to Cuba to find a man named Garcia.*

Although it's been many years since Elbert Hubbard penned these words that echoed throughout the world almost at the speed of light, his point is probably more important today than it was then.

Every organization is in constant need of responsible people who will "take the message to Garcia." There are never enough of them.

Why? Why are people who will assume total responsibility so rare?

Responsibility—A Matter of Mental and Emotional Congruence

You can't just say, "Okay, I'll get results." It takes the congruence of several mental and emotional traits to cause you to get results.

Following are five traits that must converge within you before you can make things happen:

1. *Specific know-how*
2. *Belief in abilities*
3. *Character*
4. *Willingness to act*
5. *Commitment to results*

As you think of these five traits, let me emphasize that bringing them into congruence gives you the mental and emotional powers to get results. Let's look at how this is shown in the "Responsibility Congruence Model," below.

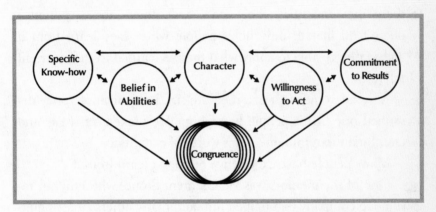

Responsibility Congruence Model

As you examine this model, let me make these points.

1. *Where gaps exist between the dimensions, conflicts occur and low productivity will result.*
2. *Each dimension or trait is necessary for the best results to occur.*
3. *As the traits are developed, your ability to get results will expand.*
4. *The convergence of these traits isn't an issue of knowing about them. It takes place deep within your "I Am" dimension.*

Let's think about each of these.

Specific Know-How

I use the term "know-how" to mean more than mere knowledge, although it includes that. It's really knowledge plus the specific skills of *applying* that knowledge. Some folks say that a person has "street smarts" or is "game-wise." Boxers call it "ring savvy."

Specific know-how is developed as we learn from experience. We can have a lot of experience but still be lacking in *know-how*, because we haven't chosen to learn from it. Here's where many people get confused—they think that years of experience give them the credentials they need to do their jobs. Experience doesn't do that. It only helps people when they learn from it and as they're able to apply what they've learned in their current job roles.

A friend, a manager of a medium-sized organization, once described one of his people by saying, "He's taken ten years and crammed them into one year's worth of experience."

Many people have experience but don't learn from it.

One of my mentors was W. Clement Stone, who built an insurance company that helped him and many others amass significant wealth. He taught me a lot about this subject of *know-how*. He also called this trait "activity knowledge," or knowing how to do the activities that lead to successful results.

Mr. Stone taught me that learning is more than knowing facts; it's the ability to extract the principles involved in getting results. He talked a great deal about how *know-how* is learning the particular skills that make things happen. It's the proper application of knowledge. *Know-how* is developed by consistently learning from our experiences.

My objective in writing this book is to present to you communication, problem-solving, and career-enhancing processes and then to encourage you to develop *know-how* by taking action and applying these strategies. The formula is this:

Knowledge + Application + Learning from
experience = Know-how

DEVELOPING SPECIFIC KNOW-HOW

Developing know-how begins with your desire to be more effective. To get more done. To be highly respected by your peers and superiors. To enjoy greater rewards from your career. To be seen by others as a *gets-it-done* person. You must have a compelling reason that creates the desire to be more effective, or you'll stay where you are.

My question to you is this: "What do you want to enjoy in your life that assuming greater responsibility and getting higher results will bring you?"

If you can't answer my question quickly, or if your answer is "nothing," then you're not mentally or emotionally ready to move ahead. But if your answer is "I want to enjoy new goals and achieve higher success because of specific rewards they'll bring me," then you're ready to move on.

A desire for the better things of life—however you define them—is necessary, or you'll not expend the effort and run the risks that accompany greater responsibility. A conscious desire to live up to strong values can motivate you. A conviction that you've been put here to create the most value for the most people can give you push and purpose.

Here are some actions that will help you develop stronger specific *know-how.*

1. *Decide on rewards you want to enjoy that being more productive would bring you.*

2. *Write the results that you must make happen to bring you the rewards of greater compensation and respect, or value to your organization.*

3. *Seek out one or two people who are performing on a level on which you'd like to be performing. Study them. Learn from*

them. Seek their advice about what success principles they've learned.

4. Take action and apply the principles you learn.

5. Assume responsibility for results.

When you make a no-withdrawal commitment to a goal, objective, or result, and have the character to keep your promises, you'll find *ways* to reach those ends. This is how you develop *know-how*—knowing how to get things done.

Belief in Abilities

I once had a staff person who consistently volunteered for projects that demanded results. He would volunteer for anything. The problem was that he never carried through on his commitments. There was always a reason why he couldn't make things happen. Sometimes he just "didn't have enough time." Or he'd blame other people, get sick, or invent creative things "he couldn't control" as his excuses.

One of the ways he set the stage for failure was really bizarre. His job was to set up seminars, which involved telephone contacts, and then help conduct them. Each month he set higher goals than his counterparts did. Then he'd chide them for their low goals as his way of lording it over them.

As the month moved on, he'd begin to clear his throat so loudly that you could hear him all over the office. By the end of the month or the seminar date, his throat was so irritated that he croaked like a frog. So, of course, he couldn't carry through on his commitment because he couldn't speak.

This happened month after month. I confronted him once about whether this throat irritation was intentional, and he vigorously denied this was so—looking at me as if I'd lost my mind. As I began to really observe and listen to him, it became obvious to me that deep down he didn't believe he had the abilities to reach the goals that he consistently set. Rather than face this reality, and learn more skills, he relied on excuses. My guess is that his ego probably never allowed him to come to grips with his self-defeating behaviors.

Unless we deeply believe that we can reach certain goals, we'll either consciously or unconsciously torpedo ourselves. We'll find excuses for not performing.

Your belief in your abilities is almost always based on your *past experiences,* not just *current knowledge.* Successful experiences cause you to develop stronger unconscious beliefs. These help you to form new pictures in your "I Am" or to strengthen your internal programming.

Following are some practical ways of strengthening your unconscious beliefs about your abilities.

Step 1—Visualizing past successes. *Several times each day, stop and recall a time when you successfully carried out a project or reached a goal. Mentally and emotionally relive the experience. Capture the feeling of success that it gave you.*

Step 2—Frame new mental pictures. *Allow yourself a few moments to feel good about what you did. As you recall a past success, immediately think of a current goal and say to yourself, "If I reached that goal in the past, I can reach this one now!" Repeat this until you begin to unconsciously believe it.*

Step 3—Select goals, projects, jobs, or actions that are just a bit beyond your current level of achievement. *Commit yourself to making them happen; then go through Steps 1 and 2 mentioned above.*

Step 4—Reward yourself when you accomplish your new goals or commitments. *Feel good about what you accomplish.*

Practicing these four steps will help you gradually build your unconscious beliefs about what level of goals you're capable of achieving.

Remember, your beliefs in your abilities have little to do with your current knowledge. They're the result of a lifetime of pro-gramming in your unconscious "I Am" dimension. The good news is that they can be changed—if you're willing to work on them.

Again, I dangle in front of you the powerful truth—*What you feed your mind, you become.*

Character

The next part of our congruence model is character, which is made up of a person's internal values. Your values are the rules by which you run your life. They describe *who* you are. Your values determine behaviors you *will* do, and ones you *won't* do. Your val-ues define what you'll do in different situations. Will you keep going when the going gets tough? Or will you cave in?

When you make choices that are congruent with strong, posi-tive values, you trigger forces within yourself that cause you to be strong—physically, emotionally, and spiritually.

People who possess strong character keep their commitments because of their keen sense of responsibility. They carefully make promises they plan to keep and consciously keep those they make.

Strong character has a profound effect on your emotional well-being, as well as your everyday behaviors. With a solid foundation of values, you're able to handle the storms that life brings you. It gives you a moral compass that helps you maintain a course of true North.

In the language of our three-dimensional human behavior model, observe how character influences your emotions and con-scious choices.

As you study this model (see page 151), remember the process:

1. *Your conscious choices, decisions, commitments, and promises immediately interact with your values and internal program-ming.*

2. *This interaction immediately creates an emotion.*
3. *Your emotions then influence your future choices, decisions, commitments, or resolutions.*
4. *If your conscious choices are congruent with your unconscious values and beliefs, then positive, strong emotions are triggered that reinforce your resolutions. If there's a conflict, negative emotions are triggered that weaken your conscious commitments.*

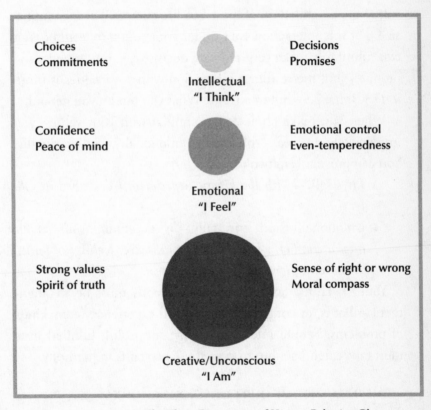

The Three Dimensions of Human Behavior: Character

You first need to choose appropriate values that lead to successful behavior. These can be revisited each day of your life. Strong character helps you live true to these values. It ensures that your conscious choices, decisions, and subsequent behavior will be congruent with them.

The strength of your character will then predict your future success, happiness, and quality of life. Your ability to lead a productive, fulfilled life can be foretold by:

- *how well you form positive inner values* and
- *how well you make choices or decisions that are congruent with these inner values.*

The degree of personal power you enjoy in your life is the result of the combination of these two life choices. Let me emphasize that this interaction isn't under your *voluntary control*. You *can* voluntarily make your choices, decisions, commitments, and promises, but the resulting interaction with your values is *involuntary*. It happens automatically. What you put in, you get out.

When you make choices that conflict with your values, you immediately go weak—physically, emotionally, and spiritually. You can prove this in two ways:

- Physically—*with the kinetic experiment I described in Chapter 6.*
- Emotionally and spiritually—*by examining your emotions after a conflict, when you'll often discover feelings of guilt, remorse, or a prevailing not-so-goodness.*

Your "I Think" and "I Am" dimensions must be in alignment—that is, in congruence—or you'll experience many kinds of problems. People intent on happy, successful, fulfilled lives must take careful actions to keep these two parts in harmony.

THE INFLUENCE OF OUR CONSCIOUS CHOICES

William James, commonly called the father of modern-day psychology, wrote this about the impact of our thinking upon our behaviors: "All mental states are followed by bodily activity of some sort, i.e., they lead to inconspicuous changes in breathing, circulation, general muscular tension, and glandular or other visceral activity."

He went on: "*All* states of mind, even mere thoughts and feelings, are *motor* in their consequences."

What he's really saying is that all thoughts and emotions have physical manifestations. When your thoughts, choices, and actions are all consistent with strong values and ethical standards, you'll enjoy strong character. This inner condition automatically infuses you with confidence, authority, and personal power.

Not only do these positive, expansive emotions saturate your entire being, they're communicated to people around you.

To summarize briefly: Every choice, decision, commitment, or promise you make has an immediate, involuntary influence upon your body, mind, and spirit. Those made out of a sense of responsibility, driven by strong character, empower you at the deepest levels within you.

Few things have more of an impact on your actual successes than these deep emotional causes. Knowledge doesn't. Circumstances don't.

Willingness to Act

The fourth part of our congruence model is your willingness to act. It's basically this: Are you willing to take action and do the necessary actions that must be done to complete a commitment you've made?

For the last twenty years, I've carried in my briefcase a little yellow dog-eared copy of a speech that Albert E. N. Gray made to the 1940 National Association of Life Underwriters Convention. Mr. Gray was the president of the Prudential Insurance Company of America. The title of this timeless booklet is *The Common Denominator of Success*.

Mr. Gray writes: *"The common denominator of success—the secret of success of every man who has ever been successful—lies in the fact that he formed the habit of doing things that failures don't like to do."*

As you mull over Mr. Gray's wisdom, forget that it was spoken many years ago and bring it forward to today. His profound advice is just as true now as it was then. Visualize him sitting in a chair next to you, talking to you personally. Shade this with the fact that he'd earned the right to share this "secret" with you. Set both of you in your current environment—whatever that is. Both of you are very comfortable. He's smiling at you and is genuinely interested in giving you the best advice he can, based on his very high level of career success.

As you capture the setting, ask yourself these questions.

1. *What are the things that successful people in my organization, career, or job do that underperforming people are unwilling to do?*
2. *Am I willing to do these things?*
3. *What do I need to know, learn, or develop in order to prepare myself to do these things?*

Your willingness to follow these suggestions will heavily influence your future success. I promise you that as soon as you begin this journey toward personal responsibility, you'll place yourself among the very few who achieve higher success.

DOING MORE THAN IS EXPECTED OF YOU

Another factor common to highly successful people is that they believe in going the *extra mile* in their jobs. They look for ways to do more than that for which they're paid.

This philosophy can take many forms. I recently received an e-mail from a participant in our "The Customer" program. In this eight-week course, we get participants doing *extra-mile* activities. One such activity we call *"I Just Caught Someone Doing Some-*

thing Right" cards. We ask people to look around during the week and notice people who do extra-effort activities and to send them a card.

One person sent another participant a *"Caught Ya!"* card saying, "You are a real team player and I appreciate your hard work. You are doing an awesome job." Not twenty minutes later he got an e-mail back from her. "She told me she was having a hard day and was really stressed, but the fact that I noticed all she did turned her day around."

He summed up the lesson he learned: "Sometimes we think people know when they're doing a good job and they don't need to be told. But guess what I learned? They do! You might even turn someone's dreary day into sunshine, and that makes me feel pretty good, and all I had to do was let someone know I noticed."

Isn't it amazing how simple, everyday expressions to people can have such an impact upon them?

What actions can you take that show you're an *extra-mile* person? What are the things that successful people do in your job or career role that unsuccessful ones aren't willing to do? Are you willing to take action and do them? What do you need to know, learn, or develop in order for you to do those things?

Commitment to Results

This is the fifth trait of our "Responsibility Congruence Model."

In my many years of conducting development courses for people, I've noticed that people fall into three categories:

1. *People who don't know what's happening.*
2. *People who wait for others to make things happen.*
3. *People who take the initiative and make things happen.*

If you were to guess, what percentage of all workers today fall into each of these three categories? How would you guess that each of these three approaches influences their self-esteem? Job stability? Compensation? Respect of others? Personal happiness? Hope for the future?

Who makes the choice about which of these three categories describes them?

IT'S A MATTER OF CONGRUENCE

Successfully getting results isn't just a voluntary choice you make. It begins there, but unless the other traits I've mentioned in this chapter are in congruence, you can make commitments that you may not actually carry out. *Wanting to, knowing how,* and *willingness to act* are all necessary.

The truth I share with you in this chapter can be understood and applied on many different levels. The more you learn about it, the more you learn there is to learn. The higher you go, the higher you'll discover you can go.

As we near the end of this chapter, let me pull it all together. Please go back and study the "Responsibility Congruence Model" again. Notice the five dimensions.

Please ask yourself the following questions as you review the model:

1. *Which dimensions am I strongest in?*
2. *Which ones do I need to strengthen?*
3. *What conflicts do I have between these traits?*
4. *What actions can I take to bring these traits into congruence within me?*

Asking these questions will help you discover actions you can take to strengthen your traits. But just knowing isn't enough. You must take action and apply the suggestions I gave you in this chapter. Let me emphasize that the congruence of these traits only happens *experientially*—only as you apply these principles that I share with you.

RESULTS ARE WHAT COUNTS

A mentor of mine, a man who started with nothing and acquired and gave away hundreds of millions of dollars, had a saying: *Results are what count.* The higher you aspire to achieve, and the higher you climb in your career ladder, the more necessary it is for you to get specific, measurable results.

My question to you is this: Are you emotionally and mentally ready to assume greater responsibility for getting results? I gotta be honest with you and tell you that the more responsibility you assume, the more stress and risk you'll encounter. But these are necessary for you to enjoy the higher rewards that will surely come as a result.

The more results you can make happen, the higher your value to your organization will be. Also, the more you can work through other people to get higher results, the greater your success will eventually be.

What's your decision? What actions do you need to take to strengthen the five traits I've written about in this chapter? How committed are you to taking those actions?

Will you be the one who steps forward and volunteers to "take the message to Garcia"?

HOW TO GAIN THE MOST FROM THIS CHAPTER

The Greek philosopher Democritus, living from 460 to 370 B.C., penned some very wise words when he wrote this: *"Nature and education are somewhat similar. The latter transforms man, and in so doing creates a second nature."*

A "second nature" is an elevated one that can lead us step-by-step to unlimited levels of achievement and quality of life. The "nature" within us that assumes responsibility for results is usually a developed one. You move up to higher levels of career success by making more happen.

In this chapter I've shared with you five traits that must be brought into congruence within you in order for you to get higher results.

1. *Specific know-how*
2. *Belief in abilities*
3. *Character*
4. *Willingness to act*
5. *Commitment to results*

These traits are not gained by knowledge or education, but *rather are developed as you learn from experience.*

I've shared actions and thinking strategies that, when practiced in the stream of your life, will gradually help you strengthen your ability to take responsibility for results. I've suggested that you sit down and define your desired level of success—income, job level, quality of life, or career fulfillment—and then carefully define the results you'll need to make happen in order to enjoy these rewards.

I also challenged you to adopt this personal credo: *I do the things that unsuccessful people are unwilling to do!*

Repeat this self-suggestion thousands of times until it's indelibly woven through the fabric of your unconscious values and self-beliefs.

Practice my ideas with patience, and you'll soon begin to see and feel changes in your personal and career success. Your conscious choices, aligning themselves with your unconscious values and self-beliefs, will form your character; and this will determine your future success.

Self-Assessment: Assume Responsibility

Take a moment to read each of the following statements. Then circle the number that best describes your actions or thoughts, with *1* being "Never" and *10* being "Always."

1. I'm constantly developing the traits that cause success in my field.

   1   2   3   4   5   6   7   8   9   10

2. I continually learn from seasoned, wise people who know my business or field.

   1   2   3   4   5   6   7   8   9   10

3. I spend time daily visualizing past successes to build confidence in my abilities.

   1   2   3   4   5   6   7   8   9   10

4. I keep my mind open to developing new skills and abilities.

   1   2   3   4   5   6   7   8   9   10

5. I always make decisions and take actions that are consistent with my values.

   1   2   3   4   5   6   7   8   9   10

6. I never violate my values and beliefs about what's right.

   1   2   3   4   5   6   7   8   9   10

7. I am extremely conscientious and diligent in getting things done.

   1   2   3   4   5   6   7   8   9   10

8. Once I know what to do, I take quick action.

   1   2   3   4   5   6   7   8   9   10

9. When I make a commitment, I keep it.

   1   2   3   4   5   6   7   8   9   10

10. I have a strong sense of accountability.

   1   2   3   4   5   6   7   8   9   10

Action Guide: *Daily Success Diary*

Assume Responsibility

Please score yourself from 1 to 10 for each daily activity, with *1* being "Never" and *10* being "Always."

	S	M	T	W	T	F	S
1. I learned from an experience today.							
2. I observed a wise, successful person today.							
3. I consciously set a daily success goal and achieved it.							
4. I visualized a past success today.							
5. I consciously thought about my values today.							
6. I made decisions that were congruent with my values.							
7. I did something that I didn't want to do but needed to do.							
8. I did an extra-mile action today.							
9. I focused on result-producing activities rather than tension-relieving ones.							
10. I carried through on a previous commitment.							
Total each day							

I know you believe you understand what you think I said, but I'm
not sure you realize that what you heard is not what I meant to say.

(Anonymous)

8 Listen to Customers

Understand Who People Are
and How They Think

"I will openly admit that my listening skills are challenging," wrote
one of our course participants. "For the most part I'm always looking for the *Reader's Digest* version. Just give me the details that I
need to know, and I'll ask the questions if I don't understand."

The *Reader's Digest* mode of listening describes many people.

Has anyone ever interrupted you before you could finish a sentence? Or stopped you and informed you what they think you're
about to say? Or allowed his eyes to drift northeasterly, telling you
that he's reliving last Saturday's golf game? Or have you ever told
someone something only to hear her retell it with a totally different meaning?

Do we really listen to people? Do we intentionally listen to what
customers *say*? To what they *mean*? How they *feel*? Who they *are*?

How many people from whom you buy things really listen to
you? How does it make you feel when they do? Or when they
don't? What do you emotionally feel when people carefully and
cautiously listen to you? How do you feel about them? How do

you feel about yourself? Does their sincere act of listening ever influence your decision to purchase from them?

What do you do when you actively listen to another person? What level of personal effectiveness and influence does it give you? How does it separate you from other people with whom your customers or associates interact?

I'll attempt to answer these and other questions in this chapter. Practice my advice in your career and life, and you'll suddenly place yourself in higher levels of influence.

You'll definitely stand out from other people.

Active Listening

Active listening is the fourth step of our *G. Val Hi* communication system. This week you'll practice these Action Guides:

1. *Listen to words.*
2. *Listen to tone of voice.*
3. *"Listen" to body language.*

Dr. Albert Mehrabian of the University of California at Los Angeles once wrote an article entitled "Communication Effectiveness." In it he said that communication effectiveness is

7 percent the words we say,

38 percent the way we say the words, and

55 percent our body language, gestures, and expressions.

In this chapter, we'll think of each of these areas that affect our ability to listen to people.

Listen to People's Words

Want to do a rewarding experiment? Try this on the next ten people with whom you talk. Carefully notice what percentage of the words you say to them are really heard and understood. Watch their eyes, their body language, their attention.

You'll be amazed at how few people really hear everything you say. What you'll experience are these different responses.

1. *Their eyes wander and get glazed over about halfway through your point.*
2. *They interrupt you and finish your sentences.*
3. *They interrupt you and then set about telling you what they think you meant to say.*
4. *They hear you say a word that reminds them of something, and they interrupt you and begin telling you what they thought of.*
5. *They truly listen to you and hear all the words you say.*

Do your own research. See what percentage of people really hear you. Then flip this around and ask yourself, "What percentage of other people's words do I hear?"

Listen to People's Tone of Voice

When I was a kid, we had a subculture language. We would say a word in a certain tone that communicated the opposite meaning. We knew as kids that our tone of voice communicated more than our actual spoken words.

My friend Maxine McIntyre Hammond, an excellent speaker on interpersonal communications, makes a great point about speech meanings. She first says this statement: *I never said he stole the money!*

Then she asks her audience to say this sentence six times, each time emphasizing a different word. She leads them:

- "**I** never said he stole the money."
- "I **never** said he stole the money."
- "I never **said** he stole the money."
- "I never said **he** stole the money."
- "I never said he **stole** the money."
- "I never said he stole **the money**."

See how the meaning changes with emphasis on different words? Could we unconsciously give off meanings different from what we intend?

"Listen" to People's Body Language

For many years Maxine taught communication skills to police officers and undercover agents. She learned through research that criminals unconsciously size people up before attacking them. If people walk tall and seem confident, they're less likely to be attacked. She makes the point that if we walk tall and look successful, people will unconsciously treat us with more respect. "They don't know any different," she explains.

Each of us has our own body language. It's been unconsciously developed as a result of our self-beliefs. We communicate messages both consciously and subconsciously with our body language. Understanding body language can help us to

- *interpret what we see in others* and
- *send the right message to others.*

People's body language tips us off to many facts about them. Among them are these: their level of self-esteem, their interest in you, their openness to you, their interest in what you're selling or telling them, their trust and comfort level with you.

Your own observation and intuition will teach you many lessons as you interact with people. Watch their eyes, hands, and posture, and you'll soon become a student.

As you observe others, analyze your own body language: Does it convey positive strength when you look people in the eye? Do you give them a firm handshake? And stand tall with your head held up when you walk? Open gestures with your hands and arms invite people into your space. Closed gestures keep people out and create communication barriers. Nodding approval as you listen helps you connect with others.

As you understand more about the power of your and other people's body language, you'll increase your listening skills.

Observe People's Space

If you'll carefully notice, each person with whom you communicate has his or her own need for space—a personal comfort zone. Some people want you to remain at a safe distance from them. Others enjoy close touch. Some want you to speak softly; others enjoy your outgoing personality.

Make it a point to notice how close people want you to be to them. You can tell by observing how they position themselves to you. Talkers enjoy closeness and informality. Controllers like distance—both physical and emotional separation. Doers need to dominate; they seek power positions—sitting behind a large desk or at the head of the table. Supporters will acquiesce space to you even when they're uncomfortable doing so. They won't verbally tell you that they feel invaded, but their facial expressions and body language will.

Be careful not to sit in a Doer's chair or at his or her place at a table. Don't sit or stand too close to a Controller. Don't sit too far from a Talker, or stifle your gestures or responses. Don't come on too strong or push Supporters, but be easy with them.

You'll communicate most effectively when you can understand each person's need for space and then honor it.

I must emphasize that our cultures have a lot to do with our spatial comfort levels. In one of our recent seminars, we had a mixture of Johnson & Johnson managers from Germany, France, Italy, and Spain. They were grouped at tables according to language. Their group discussions, responses, and interaction during breaks were significantly different. The Germans were aloof, skeptical, and reserved. The French were a bit more animated. The Italian and Spanish people's hands were constantly moving around. Their body language showed much more openness and intimacy. They talked louder and were much more jovial than the others.

Rather than trying to make rules for all people, we must understand different cultural values, beliefs, and accepted behaviors. But remember, when we're observant, people will tell or show us how close or far they want us to be in relation to them.

Your Ability to Be Successful

All this comes down to this simple fact: Your ability to be successful, in almost any field, depends on your ability to communicate effectively with those around you.

Unless you're a genius who takes up where Albert Einstein left off, and are so critical to some technological enterprise that people overlook your lack of interpersonal skills, you'll need to communicate well.

Communication skills involve two things:

- *Your ability to understand and relate to people.*
- *Your ability to help people understand and relate to you.*

For most of us, these are developed skills, not natural ones.

Understanding Others

A young man stood in a seminar I was conducting and, after taking three or four deep breaths, finally said, "I went home a few months ago and found my wife in bed with my best friend!" The pain in his heart and soul streaked through his words as he shared his brokenness with other participants. All of a sudden, other participants understood some of his recent behaviors.

This was the third day of a seminar for salespeople whose production had plateaued. The seminar's purpose was to help them discover their own blockages. It had taken, as always, the first two days to build a mutual trust among the participants. Then the emotional blocks began to come down. When they did, a deeper understanding, acceptance, and communication resulted.

I've listened to tens of thousands of people in development courses I've conducted. I've heard people confess to just about anything you could imagine when they bonded with the other participants and felt they could trust them. All of them had an unrealized need to tell their stories to people who would support them, listen to them, and give them unconditional acceptance. Past experiences that have festered inside people's psyches are often automatically released when they feel understood without judgment.

Everyone Has a Story

I have come to believe that everyone has a *story* that needs to be told. Our *stories* explain *why* we are *who* we are. In most cases our *stories* get locked up inside us because in the drumbeat of life there simply aren't enough people with whom we can *safely* share them.

Years ago I picked up a little book by John Powell entitled *Why Am I Afraid to Tell You Who I Am?* He began the book by telling a story of meeting a friend. His friend asked him, "John, what are you doing now?"

He told his friend, "I'm writing a book," whereupon his friend asked him, "What's the title of it?" He replied, "*Why Am I Afraid to Tell You Who I Am?*"

His friend asked, "Why *are* you afraid to tell me who you are?"

Powell replied, "Because I'm afraid you won't like who I am, and . . . I'm all I've got!"

So often, it's the inability to share our story that clogs up our emotional and spiritual arteries, and occasionally deadens our self-esteem, creativity, and views of our possibilities. To the extent that people's *stories* remain buried, something creative often dies within.

I recently conducted a four-day seminar for a group of managers. The first day, one of them was in my face at each break, not negatively, but trying to impress me with his history of success. He dominated group discussions, usually "volunteering" to be the discussion leader. He wanted everyone to know how much he earned. He liberally gave out advice. He didn't appear to be there to *learn*, but to *teach*.

It was during the third day that he became quieter, laying aside his know-it-all facade.

At the graduation, on the fourth day, the participants were asked to come to the head table and share with the group:

1. *What they gained from the seminar.*
2. *How they will put that insight into practice.*
3. *What results they expect to enjoy.*

Most of the talks centered around business, but not this person's. He stood silent for a moment, seriously collecting his thoughts, and then told *his story.*

It seemed that he and his wife had lost a child, which sent his wife into a deep, immobilizing depression. After two years, she thought that having another child would help her, so months later they did. But, rather than diminishing, her depression increased, adding to his burdens.

Then he came to the subject "What did I gain from this seminar?" He confessed that he was a poor listener. He said that his relationship with his wife was so bad that she had hardly talked to him in months and wouldn't even answer the telephone when she knew it was him. He admitted that his insecurities caused him to talk too much and exaggerate his achievement. He talked about calling home six times the night before, until his wife finally answered.

When she answered, he quickly apologized to her for not understanding her condition. He admitted that he'd been a poor listener and asked for her forgiveness. In a most contrite way, he shared that he simply listened to her for three hours, and at the end their communication had improved so much that she welcomed him home and expressed her desire to work out their challenges.

This man left the seminar a totally different person than when he entered it.

Everyone has a *story*, and a compelling need to tell it to people they trust. I've seen many people unclog their souls, strip off old constraints, and release new energies as they've shared their *stories* with people who they knew would just listen and not judge, criticize, or condemn them.

We help people when we listen. Often people's lives are transformed when we do.

Every Person Craves Understanding

Dr. Carl Rogers, father of much of modern-day nondirective counseling, emphasizes over and over that one of our highest needs is to be understood. He writes that the key to relationships, rapport, or empathy with others is gained through *accepting* them as they are—as valuable, creative human beings.

In his book *On Becoming a Person*, Rogers writes, "By acceptance I mean a warm regard for him as a person of unconditional self-worth—of value—no matter what his condition, his behavior or his feelings." He also advises, "When I accept myself as I am, I change. When I accept others as they are, they change."

I've taken this dynamic concept and designed complete personal development courses around it. After having several hundred thousand people in my courses, I've come to believe that this becomes the key for people to unlock their real creative powers as well as their dynamic personalities that have been kept locked.

Nonjudgmental listening is at the very heart of this transforming process—both for the giver and the recipient.

People Only Share Their Stories with Others They Can Trust

Before people will take the risk of revealing to us who and what they are—*their stories*—they must first know they can trust us. My experience is that often people open up less to those closest to them than they do with strangers.

My friends Dave and Nan Warren owned a furniture and home accessories consignment business in Fort Worth, Texas. It takes Nan about fifteen seconds to gain rapport with people. People start telling her their troubles in line to buy a movie ticket.

Several times while I was in their store, I noticed people just stopping by to visit. They'd tell Nan about their problems, their children's problems—everything you could think of. She is such a positive, noncondemning person that people are drawn to her so they can tell her their stories.

Literally thousands of times, in development courses I've conducted, I've heard participants preface their talks with "I've never told anyone this . . . not even my wife [or husband], but . . ."

It's here that their story comes out.

As I listened to all these people unload mental and emotional anguish, it was usually clear that they had had absolutely no previous plan to share it—they just blurted out the story because it needed to come out. This phenomenon appeared to be totally unconsciously driven.

When people felt safe, the toxic stuff poured forth.

People Silently Scream to Be Understood

People move through relationships, jobs, customer contacts—through life—silently screaming, "Please understand me! Please understand how
"*I feel;*
"*I think;*
"*I view the world;*
"*I picture myself;*
"*I perceive you;*
"*I want to be served;*
"*I want you to value me.*"
Your customers, your internal associates, your family, your friends are all silently saying to you: "Please try to understand how I see the world! You don't necessarily have to agree with me—just understand me."
But are we prepared to hear them?

We Filter Our Listening

Each of us has certain biases—unique lenses through which we see the world.
We communicate well with people who think and see the world as we do. Left to our natural instincts, we either ignore divergent thinking or we try to prove it wrong.
We constantly experience situations where we choose to accept or reject ideas of others that either fit or don't fit our own set of beliefs. Wisdom is understanding our preconceptions and how they color our thinking. It's also judiciously working through those preconceptions so they don't block our ability to understand how and why others think as they do.
Throughout this book, I'll suggest ways to move past your own biases, preconceived notions, and established paradigms of

thought. This doesn't mean you have to change any principles, values, or core beliefs; rather, it's about dropping barriers that may keep you from understanding others.

We Tend to Hear What We're Programmed to Hear

Isn't it interesting that when the president of the United States holds a news conference, two reporters can dissect it and interpret it totally differently?

But maybe we all do the same thing. How often do we feel rebuffed by a coworker or customer only to later understand that the comment or action wasn't meant to be taken personally? How often do we form opinions of other people and then allow those opinions to shade our interactions with them—only to later discover that we were wrong?

I've come to believe after listening to tens of thousands of people in my development courses that around 85 percent of everything that motivates our actions, moods, and emotional responses is the result of past conditioning and developed beliefs. To make quick judgments of customers, or people with whom we work, can lead to many misunderstandings.

It cuts both ways. How many of us, if we had our toast burned in the morning or were cut off by a maniac on the freeway or were worried about paying our bills, allowed these incidents to influence our response to customers? Usually, that's the day customers are the most demanding and difficult—or so it seems.

One way to effectively understand people is to realize we're all different. We don't make decisions the same way, nor are we motivated for the same reasons. We all perceive the world differently.

But there's a better way to understand the diverse traits of people.

Understanding Behavior Styles

Let's look again at a framework for understanding yourself as well as other people—the "Behavior Styles Model."

Once you identify different people's behavior styles, along with how your natural style might interact with theirs, you can adjust your thinking and responses to be customer-focused. As we focus on listening, please remember these descriptions of people.

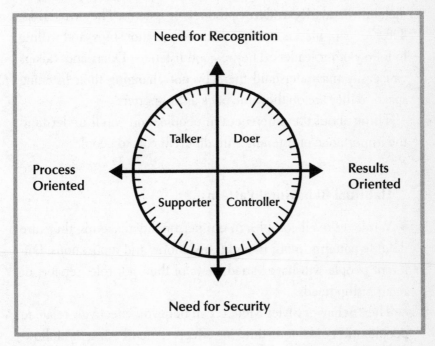

Behavior Styles Model

Talkers are friendly, social, easy-to-get-to-know people. They like people, love conversation, and value relationships. They crave recognition and attention that shows you like them. They like to be listened to, but aren't usually good listeners themselves.

Doers are achievement-oriented, results-focused, and make-it-happen people. They value power and powerful people. They require recognition for their accomplishments. Ask questions about how they became so successful, then listen, and you'll gain lasting rapport.

Controllers are logical, analytical, no-nonsense people. They respect accuracy, organization, and clear thinking. They respond to facts, proof, and data to back up your claims. They're usually good listeners. They also have great memories and will quickly sense how well you listen to and understand them.

Supporters are steady, dependable, loyal people. They need predictability and tried-and-true products or systems. They avoid risks. They're team players, noncombative in relationships, and willing to follow other leaders. They're good listeners. Doers and Talkers can easily misunderstand them by not changing their listening speed so they are on the same track as Supporters.

Think about the differences in people, and you'll understand the importance of listening with different ears to people.

Habitual Behavioral Patterns

While we're all complex in our personality makeups, there are definite patterns in our thoughts, reactions, and motivations. Different people will have varied views of their job role, service, or relationship needs.

The "Behavior Styles Model" can help you effectively relate to people and guide your thinking. Keep remembering the following suggestions as you deepen your understanding of people's styles.

1. *People are usually a combination of two styles, with one being stronger.*
2. *Usually the combinations are contiguous styles. For example, a person could be a Doer/Controller or a Controller/Doer or a Talker/Supporter or a Supporter/Controller, and so on.*
3. *More complex people are often a combination of three styles.*

4. *People with different styles can often miscommunicate with each other because they each see the world through different emotional and intellectual lenses.*

5. *Rapport is developed when we adapt our styles to fit those of other people.*

6. *Customers, or people whom we serve, need for us to communicate the way they do.*

As you understand the "Behavior Styles Model" and observe other people's actions, speech, energy levels, and reactions, you'll become more aware of their differences.

With time and practice you'll understand more and more about your own style, as well as how and why you interact with others the way you do.

More Ways to Understand People

Look at our "Behavior Styles Model" mainly as a framework for listening to and understanding people, rather than a psycho-analytic one. You're not trying to "figure out" people; you simply want to understand them so you can communicate most effectively.

Here are some ways you can listen to and understand people.

Their energy level: *Talkers and Doers have higher energy levels than Supporters and Controllers.*

Their tone of voice: *Talkers and Doers usually speak louder and more animatedly than people with other styles do.*

Their dress and grooming: *Supporters and Controllers generally are more conservative; Talkers and Doers, more flamboyant.*

Their facial expressions: *Controllers and Supporters reveal less in facial expressions and in their body language. Doers and Talkers make more eye contact, use more facial expressions, and more often use their hands to communicate than people with other styles do.*

Their trust and respect: *Talkers and Supporters generally are more trusting than Doers and Controllers. Doers usually appear more dominating and assertive, while Controllers are more skeptical and distant.*

Their need for information: *Controllers and Supporters seek more explanation and information before making decisions. They want to know why and how. Doers want proof, and Talkers are interested in who else likes it.*

What they talk about: *Doers are in a hurry and talk about results. Talkers talk about people and usually aren't in a hurry unless they have a social engagement to attend. Controllers talk about details and what could go wrong. Supporters talk about safety and possible recurring risks.*

Understanding How You Might Appear to Others

The flip side of understanding others' communication styles is being aware of your own. There'll be people with whom you naturally relate well, while your style may conflict with those of other people.

Here are some quick ideas about how you may naturally interact with other people's styles.

1. *You are a Doer interacting with:*

   a. *Controllers—They'll be more interested in the process, whereas you're more interested in the outcome. They may frustrate you by not seeing the "picture" as quickly as you do, and bore you with details.*

   b. *Supporters—You'll frustrate them, and be frustrated by them, by your differences in initiative and decision styles. You may tend to run over them.*

   c. *Talkers—You may expect decisions or actions to happen quickly, and become impatient with their need for social ap-*

proval. You want to get things done and move on; they want to talk and enjoy you.

  d. Doers—Your egos can clash and you may experience some tugs-of-war. You may want to impress them with your achievements, rather than allowing them to impress you. You may fight for "ego shelf space" with them.

2. You are a Controller interacting with:

  a. Supporters—You may be more interested in efficient processes that produce certain outcomes, where they may only be concerned with doing the process well. You may be less flexible and more critical than they are.

  b. Talkers—You may cause them to feel you don't approve of them because you're logical and reserved in your speech. They may interpret your lack of emotional display as not accepting them.

  c. Doers—You may not trust their decisions and opinions because they seem to arrive at them too quickly and without enough careful thought. You must understand and communicate about their goals and objectives rather than the process.

  d. Controllers—You'll see the world the same way, although both of you, being analytical and critical, may disagree on the facts, data, or process. The question will be "Who's right and who's wrong?"

3. You are a Supporter interacting with:

  a. Talkers—You'll be more serious than they are. You may assume they have the same needs and motivations as you do. You need to understand they'll be less conscientious about doing their jobs well than you are. You'll need to boost your energy when communicating with them.

  b. Doers—You'll need to be more direct and realize that they move, think, and act more quickly than you do. You can eas-

ily bore them with too much information. You must allow them to impress you with their achievements.

c. *Controllers—They are as detail-oriented as you, but for different reasons. You want to do your job well; they want to get results through efficiency and organization. You're conscientious; they're analytical and critical.*

d. *Supporters—You'll naturally get along and communicate well. Listen to them because their need for safety and security may not be expressed in the same way as yours is.*

4. *You are a Talker interacting with:*

a. *Doers—You may unconsciously talk too much, rather than listen to them. You may not move fast enough to connect with their style. You'll want to talk about people; they'll want to talk results or achievement.*

b. *Controllers—You'll be on a totally different wavelength. They may not think you are logical and factual enough. You may feel they don't like you. You need social approval; they don't. They need logic, facts, and distance.*

c. *Supporters—You'll connect in several ways. You may not understand their need for safety and security. They want to eliminate risks; you want them to like you.*

d. *Talkers—You'll see the world in the same way, but may butt heads to see who gets to talk the most. You may be so socially engaged that you fail to move along to a specific resolution or sale.*

These are quick ideas about how you might understand, interact, and communicate with other styles.

Remember that we're all combinations of two styles, occasionally three, so this adds some complexity to the process. With these basic ideas, you'll at least have a framework to begin understanding others and of course yourself, too.

So, whomever you serve—internal or external customers,

friends, or family members—you can now begin to shift your natural style to blend with their styles.

Rapport—Tuning Into Each Person

Rapport is getting on the same mental and emotional wavelength with others. It's sensing how people want to communicate, then shifting from your style to theirs. Great communicators seem to instinctively understand this. Most of us have to learn it. Not only learn it, but then consciously develop unconscious habits of *doing* it.

Let me make a simple point before we move on. It seems to me that in serving others, whatever role that takes, there are three viewpoints we can have:

1. *It's all about* me.
2. *It's all about* you.
3. *It's all about* us.

An *us* connection is the most healthy, fulfilling, and ultimately successful one. It promotes long-term relationships, as well as building trust and confidence in both parties—each person respects and feels good about the other.

As I've mentioned before, for many years I had a business partner, Bernard Petty. He and his wife, Laverne, had one of the best marriages I've ever seen. It dawned on me one day that there were basically two reasons why it was so strong. First, he got up each day with a total goal of making her happy. And she got up each day with the single purpose of making him happy.

Consequently, both had their relationship needs filled. Neither ever asked, "What have you done for me lately?" Both asked, "What can I do for you today?"

But the thing that made their relationship work so well was the flip side of it. Each allowed the other to *give* to them. Paradoxically, we can best serve others when they graciously allow us to do so.

Relationships have two sides.

- "*My objective is to fill your needs.*"
- "*My other objective is to allow you to fill mine.*"

This reciprocity is necessary for healthy relationships, whether they're personal or business.

It's not just about *you*, or *me*, but *us*.

To Be Understood, First Understand

"Empathetic listening is always centered on the other person, and its goal is to make the other feel uniquely understood," wrote Arthur P. Ciaramicoli in his excellent book *The Power of Empathy.*

Similarly, Emerson noted this truth: "It's a luxury to be understood."

Since all of us have a deep need to be understood, we achieve it and deserve it when we understand others.

HOW TO GAIN THE MOST FROM THIS CHAPTER

In this chapter you learned that everyone craves understanding and that we serve people best when we truly want to understand their needs, wants, or objectives. You also learned that we hear what we're programmed to hear.

We suggested three Action Guides for listening to customers:

1. *Listen to people's words.*
2. *Listen to people's tone of voice.*
3. *Listen to people's body language.*

Allow some time to read, reread, and digest this chapter. You may want to review the "Behavior Styles Model" more than once. Understand the differences in the styles.

In your day-to-day interactions with people, try the following actions:

1. *Understand your own natural style.*
2. *Carefully listen to people and observe how they talk, move, think, and see the world.*
3. *After each contact, take a moment to review what you observed in each person. Ask yourself how you could have adapted to their style.*
4. *Take on the other person's feelings, viewpoints, and emotional tone as much as possible.*

After a while you'll learn to do these actions unconsciously. As you do, you'll enjoy a new level of confidence and communication effectiveness. People will be more naturally drawn to you. Your service skills will stand out. You'll answer one of your customers' or associates' greatest needs: to be understood.

And then, quite serendipitously, you'll receive understanding back—which you deserve to enjoy.

Self-Assessment: *Listen to Customers*

Take a moment to read each of the following statements. Then circle the number that best describes your actions or thoughts, with *1* being "Never" and *10* being "Always."

1. I carefully study people's body language.

   1   2   3   4   5   6   7   8   9   10

2. I'm always careful not to crowd people's personal space.

   1   2   3   4   5   6   7   8   9   10

3. I listen to people's tone of voice to determine their meaning.

   1   2   3   4   5   6   7   8   9   10

4. I listen to people without judging their motives.

   1   2   3   4   5   6   7   8   9   10

5. I always listen more than I talk.

   1   2   3   4   5   6   7   8   9   10

6. I always allow people to finish their thoughts before I speak.

   1   2   3   4   5   6   7   8   9   10

7. I clearly understand my own behavior style.

   1   2   3   4   5   6   7   8   9   10

8. I always adjust my communication style to those of others.

   1   2   3   4   5   6   7   8   9   10

9. I always take on other people's feelings and emotional tone.

   1   2   3   4   5   6   7   8   9   10

10. People consider me an excellent communicator.

   1   2   3   4   5   6   7   8   9   10

Action Guide: *Daily Success Diary*

Listen to Customers

Please score yourself from 1 to 10 for each daily activity, with *1* being "Never" and *10* being "Always."

	S	M	T	W	T	F	S
1. I listened to people's words.							
2. I listened to people's tone of voice.							
3. I "listened" to people's body language.							
4. I observed people's behavior styles and how they want me to listen to them.							
Total each day							

We are apt to forget that we are only one of a team, that in unity there is strength and that we are strong only as each unit in our organization functions with precision. (Samuel J. Tilden)

9 Practice Teamwork

Multiply Your Own
Personal Power

When I was a kid, my mother used a laundry detergent called 20 Mule Team Borax. I daydreamed for hours, looking at the illustration on the front of the box. It showed twenty mules pulling two huge wagons, plus a smaller wagon hooked behind. That picture conjured up all kinds of visions in my mind.

It was years before I learned of the significance of the picture.

It seems that in the Death Valley of California, in the 1840s, a mineral called *borax* was mined. For years it took twelve mules to pull one massive wagon of it out of a pit and to a rail head.

One day a creative thinker, probably seen by his co-workers as a dreamer and ne'er-do-well, added eight mules to the twelve. He discovered that by this addition he could pull *two* of the huge wagons, plus a water wagon.

He proved that 12 + 8 more than doubled the previous power.

Of course, there's a name for this power—*synergism*. It means that when two or more people or forces work together in a spirit of harmony, toward a common goal or purpose, the result is much more than the sum of the individual powers.

So, 2 + 2 may equal 6 or 8. Or in dysfunctional relationships, 2 + 2 may equal 1. Or minus 3!

How many teams have you seen where highly talented individuals each had his or her own different agenda? How effective were they? Contrast them with a group of people who all work together toward a common goal in a spirit of unity and harmony. The latter will almost always win.

The sports world will talk for years about the mighty Los Angeles Lakers basketball team of 2004. Not only did the team have four all-stars, but they would definitely become Hall of Fame players—Shaquille O'Neal, Kobe Bryant, Gary Payton, and Karl Malone. With that talent they seemed unstoppable. But the lowly Detroit Pistons humiliated them in the play-offs.

How could that happen?

The Pistons, minus the gigantic egos of the Lakers, seemed to subordinate their own need for glory to the good of the team. And . . . the rest is history.

The Superiority of Group Decisions

Dan Goleman, writing in his book *Primal Leadership*, emphasizes these points about the power of teams.

> In the last few decades much research has proven the superiority of group decision making over that of even the brightest individuals in the group. There is one exception to this rule. If the group lacks harmony or the ability to cooperate, decision-making quality and speed suffer.
>
> Research at Cambridge University found that even groups comprising brilliant individuals will make bad decisions if the

group disintegrates into bickering, interpersonal rivalry, or power plays.

So, the question for effective teams is "Can each person function in a spirit of unity and harmony toward common goals, and at the same time honor divergent thinking?"

You Can't Get There Alone

Wherever "there" is for you, you can't get there alone. Unless, of course, your "there" is to be a beachcomber or a hermit on a lone mountain, away from people.

The Ritz-Carlton Hotel in Phoenix discovered the power of *synergy* in a most unusual way. Typically, hotel rooms are cleaned by one person; then a floor supervisor checks on how well each room has been cleaned. In their quest for quality improvement, they asked the maids how they thought they could improve their work. As is often the case, the people who were doing the actual cleaning knew more about the process than did their managers.

The maids suggested two changes:

- *That they be allowed to work in teams of two rather than by themselves.*
- *That the floor supervisor position be eliminated and that they take responsibility for their jobs being done right.*

The maids were allowed to try their suggestions, and to select their own team members. Some new teams were mothers and daughters, and others were sisters or friends.

Immediately, quality improved. The rooms got cleaned 40 percent faster than before. Significantly, not only did this 40 percent increase reduce costs, but the savings of not having supervisors added to the efficiency.

As these savings were enjoyed, the people showed better attitudes and self-esteem. Their pride in their work increased, which contributed to job satisfaction and higher retention.

A new level of team energy was created.

Teamwork—The Creation of Energy

Energy is the driver of all achievement. There are many different levels of individual human energy that are released according to the nobility of our purpose. The hope of reward releases this energy. Sustained energy is strengthened by positive emotions of hope, love, joy, forgiveness, peace of mind, and the thrill of creating value for others. This positive kind of energy leads us to high achievement, personal fulfillment, and a sense of self-respect. It's also transferred to people around us.

Positive energy releases endorphins, chemicals found in the brain, which overcome fatigue and often leave us in a state of euphoria rather than stress.

Negative energy is released when we're fighting for survival or are pushed into doing things we either don't want to do or feel bad about doing. Fear motivation causes this negative energy. This destructive energy is often in the form of adrenaline, which can cause a burst of energy that is usually short-lived. It can also leave us more stressed than before.

It's clear that certain emotions automatically cause either positive or negative energy. While we can't control the involuntary interaction that produces emotions, we can influence their cause by our thinking. Positive thoughts lead to positive energy, and negative ones destroy or cancel group energy. The following "Causes of Energy" illustration shows the states of mind that cause each form of energy.

Not only do our own choices, or thinking patterns, determine

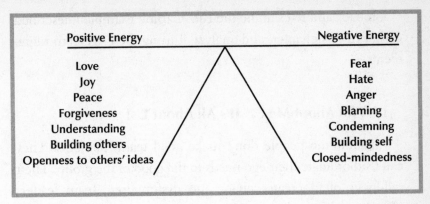

Positive Energy	Negative Energy
Love	Fear
Joy	Hate
Peace	Anger
Forgiveness	Blaming
Understanding	Condemning
Building others	Building self
Openness to others' ideas	Closed-mindedness

Causes of Energy

our energy levels; those people whom we're around also influence it. Think for a moment about specific people who influence you. Do they drain you, or do they lift you?

So, what attitudes and behaviors does it take to create new positive energy within teams?

The Anatomy of a Vibrant Team

Here are some ingredients of high-functioning teams.

1. *A goal, vision, or purpose to increase, serve, or create value for customers or other stakeholders.*
2. *A well-defined strategy for attaining the objectives that's congruent with well-entrenched core values.*
3. *Selection of the right people who have the appropriate values, work ethics, and customer focus, people who are willing to subordinate their own ego needs to the good of the group.*
4. *A clear definition of how each person's job role fits into the team's purpose.*
5. *Measurement of results and accountability.*
6. *Celebrating and rewarding performance.*

Go back and re-examine the Ritz-Carlton example I described earlier in this chapter, and analyze it using these six team ingredients.

It's Not About Me . . . It's All About Us!

All-about-me people don't make good team members. They can't subordinate their ego needs to the good of the group. Their self-focus often creates chaos and dysfunction. Team leaders often have different personality styles than team members, but to be effective, both need to understand the dynamics of teamwork.

Talkers and Supporters make good team members. Doers and Controllers often do best in leadership or management roles. All can function well when their objective is to be all-about-us people.

All-about-us people are great team players because they're energized by working together with other like-minded people. They value relationships and need the social touch and camaraderie that working together with others gives them. While everyone needs personal recognition, much of their payoff comes from being accepted by their team members. This intrinsic gratification motivates them and causes them to enjoy their work.

All-about-me people are usually self-focused. They want individual recognition, personal rewards, the trappings of success. They need trophies, awards, and visual evidence of their success placed or hung around them. They often don't make good team members.

While all of us need recognition, it's the way we want to get it that often determines whether we're team players or not.

A Great Team Model

As we think of the anatomy of a team, let's look at a common sports metaphor.

Take a moment to go back to your high school or college days and think about one of your school's athletic teams. What caused it to be successful? Or not so successful? Think for a moment of these elements.

- A name and a uniform—*an identity, a uniquely crafted distinction that differentiated them from other teams.*
- A purpose—*to win games and bring honor and recognition to their school.*
- A coach—*to set the vision, to train, and to communicate a belief that goals will be reached.*
- Captains—*leaders who understand the goals of both coaches and players and lead players by example.*
- Players—*a group of people with diverse skills and abilities who are yielding their own glory to the success of the team.*
- Basic training and conditioning—*to equip players to know what and how to perform their functions.*
- A game plan—*clear action statements that, if executed properly, should lead to victory.*
- Coaching and practice—*performance inspection and continual development of each individual's skills.*
- Scores and statistics—*specific measurements that tell the team how they're doing.*
- Rewards—*sharing the thrill of victory and the responsibility of continual learning and improvement.*

Take this metaphor and overlay it on your own team or the group of people with whom you work. See how many of these points you can apply.

Relationship Quadrants

Ideally, team members have a healthy balance of these two values:

- *"I value you as an important, creative person."*
- *"I value me as an important, creative person."*

	High		
		1 Subservience: "I don't value me, but I value you!"	**2** Balance: "I value you, and I value me, too!"
"I feel good about you"		**3** Inferiority: "I don't value you, and I don't value me, either!"	**4** Arrogance: "I value me, but I don't value you!"
	Low		High

"I feel good
about me"

Relationship Quadrants

Look at the "Relationship Quadrants" illustration above. How does the interplay of these two views of yourself and others influence your ability to function as a team?

To function best in almost any life situation, a steady move into Quadrant 2 is necessary. This emotional balance is the healthiest one. Mull over the following descriptions of each of these two *values*.

"I VALUE YOU!"
- *"I look for strengths in you."*
- *"I see potential in you."*
- *"I want to understand you."*
- *"I want you to succeed."*
- *"I can look past your flaws and focus on your good traits."*
- *"I want to lift you up."*
- *"I'm interested in your well-being."*
- *"I value your ideas."*
- *"I listen to you."*
- *"I give you credit when credit is due."*

beliefs to be formed within you that have largely influenced your current level of success, self-esteem, and quality of life.

Meditate on and accept this truth, because *it is the truth*.

Then say to yourself, "The realities of my yesterdays don't have to be the realities of my todays!"

Say this a dozen or so times. Write it down several times.

What emotions do you experience when you say this?

Okay, now I realize that just saying this and writing it down is only a *mental exercise* and will not immediately change how you *feel*. But when you do the following activities, over a period of time, your feelings and perceptions will begin to gradually change.

Moving into Quadrant 2

Here's what you can actually do to condition your inner beliefs so that you gradually move into Quadrant 2.

1. *Put a marker between the pages where the twenty "I value you" and "I value me, too" statements are printed.*
2. *Refer to the list daily, each day selecting two actions to focus on that day.*
   a. *Write on a card one statement from the "I value you" list, and write an action that puts this thought into practice.*
   b. *Write one action from the "I value me, too" list, and write an action you can take to practice it.*
3. *Practice these actions or remind yourself of the suggestions each chance you have that day.*

Will magic happen immediately? No, of course not. But as you do these actions each day, you'll begin to notice changes in your relationships with others, as well as changes in how you feel about yourself.

Here's how it works. Your conscious choice in your "I Think" to take action will interact with the values and self-esteem in your

"I VALUE ME, TOO!"

- *"I can depend on myself."*
- *"I keep my commitments."*
- *"I allow myself to feel good about my achievements."*
- *"I'm comfortable with my values."*
- *"I allow my results and actions to speak for themselves."*
- *"I allow myself to be rewarded when rewards are due."*
- *"I set goals with a quiet air of confidence that I will rea them."*
- *"I know that I'll succeed to the extent that I help my team or o ganization succeed."*
- *"I measure my own success by the value I create for others."*
- *"I have a quiet confidence about my abilities because of my strong, positive values."*

As you reflect on these twenty qualities, please go back and meditate on each one. How do you rate yourself?

Evaluating Your Team Effectiveness

You're the main team member over which you have control. Your example can influence others.

Review the above "I value you" and "I value me, too" beliefs with the knowledge that it's okay to still have room for growth. Here are some suggestions to help you.

Give yourself an emotional break and accept yourself where you are now. Breathe deeply and say, "I am who and what I currently am." Accept that fact. Then say, "I am what and who I am because of past conditioning, environment, heredity, and other factors, and I can't change the past."

Stop and spend time on this fact—you can't change the past. Mentally release yourself from old, outdated conditioning. Realize that your accumulated life perceptions have caused certain

"I Am" dimension. This will then produce positive emotions in your "I Feel." These repeated positive emotions will eventually coagulate with your "I Am," forming new inner beliefs. After this transaction is repeated hundreds of times, over a period of several weeks, your inner beliefs about *who* you are and *what* you're capable of achieving will slowly expand.

The net result of this self-programming will be that you'll move farther into Quadrant 2.

Oh yes, one other important point: The farther you move northeast into Quadrant 2, the more you'll discover possibilities for further learning and growing. You'll never reach "there," but your growth and success are measured by your continual journey toward "there."

Relationship Attitudes and Values

What attitudes and values provide predictable positive results in teamwork? As a team member, ask yourself these questions.

1. *What attitudes do I need to exhibit?*
2. *What role do I play in my team's success?*
3. *What will I gain from the relationship if:*
    a. *My main motive is what I get out of it?*
    b. *My objective is to contribute to the overall effectiveness?*

With these questions in mind, take a look at the "Relationship Attitudes and Values" model shown on page 196.

Which of the two extremes in the illustration creates the most energy? Which tends to tear teams down? Which lifts them up?

You can estimate the actual power and effectiveness of your team, whatever your objectives are, by

- *the extent to which members sincerely subscribe to constructive attitudes and values* and
- *the degree or intensity of their commitment to these attitudes and values.*

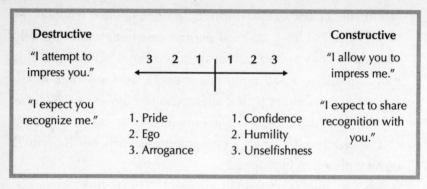

Destructive							Constructive
"I attempt to impress you."		3 2 1	1 2 3				"I allow you to impress me."
"I expect you recognize me."	1. Pride		1. Confidence				"I expect to share recognition with you."
	2. Ego		2. Humility				
	3. Arrogance		3. Unselfishness				

Relationship Attitudes and Values

Here's a quick comparison of the two opposing attitudes and values. Assume that the negative energy emitted by destructive actions cancels out the positive energy of constructive ones. Think of two specific people with whom you've worked—one positive and one negative. Then run through this evaluation. In the destructive statements, for person 1, place a dot at the point you'd evaluate him or her, and an X for person 2. Then do the same for the constructive statements. Add up the destructive scores and the constructive scores, and arrive at the difference.

DESTRUCTIVE

1. **Expects to control the group.**

   LOW   HIGH
   1   2   3   4   5   6   7   8   9   10

2. **Is opinionated.**

   LOW   HIGH
   1   2   3   4   5   6   7   8   9   10

3. **Takes credit for results.**

   LOW   HIGH
   1   2   3   4   5   6   7   8   9   10

4. **Doesn't listen to others with an open mind.**

   LOW   HIGH
   1   2   3   4   5   6   7   8   9   10

5. Dominates discussions.

LOW   HIGH

1   2   3   4   5   6   7   8   9   10

Person 1 Total _____

Person 2 Total _____

Total Negative Energy _____

CONSTRUCTIVE

1. Listens intently to others without interruption.

LOW   HIGH

1   2   3   4   5   6   7   8   9   10

2. Thinks and speaks in terms of "we" rather than "I."

LOW   HIGH

1   2   3   4   5   6   7   8   9   10

3. Gives honor and credit to others.

LOW   HIGH

1   2   3   4   5   6   7   8   9   10

4. Draws others out to understand their positions.

LOW   HIGH

1   2   3   4   5   6   7   8   9   10

5. Seeks the good of the group over self-interest.

LOW   HIGH

1   2   3   4   5   6   7   8   9   10

Person 1 Total _____

Person 2 Total _____

Total Positive Energy _____

What did you learn from the evaluation of these people?

Real-World Application

In our "The Customer" program, an eight-week course to help organizations better serve their customers, Session 6 is entitled "Building Team Synergism."

One recent participant shared this comment: "I think negativity can be like a virus and can easily be passed around." Another participant gave this report: "The thing that makes this team successful is that we work on getting the customers what they need in a fast, friendly manner."

He went on, "I have committed to having a friendly attitude and promoting team play and encouraging those with whom I work. In doing this, I am more popular with my coworkers than I have been before. More people are coming to me with questions and help. I am willing to hear them out and at least understand where they're coming from. This has helped team morale in many cases."

Another participant, with a financial services company, reported this increase in work done. "My team got an additional 600 claims to review and close. We already had 4,100 claims to process. It was amazing that we were able to get those done in a week. Working together has certainly raised the bar for us."

Another member said, "I never feel alone because I can always call on a wonderful team member to help. I came here from a job with no team and am sometimes overwhelmed with how well things go by working with this team. We are so close. One of our members' husbands came home from [military service in] Iraq. Her co-workers all told her how thrilled they were for his safe return. It was like they all were family. A box of tissues was the most popular item on the table as the tears flowed from all eyes. It made me realize the importance of a team and how our support both for job and life can make us stronger."

Do the attitudes and values I present in this book work in the real world? These and thousands of our course graduates from whom we hear certainly seem to answer a resounding "yes!"

In team synergy, what influences one member affects them all. As team rapport increases, many factors—both on and off the job—either bring them together or separate them. As teams move to deeper relationships, more of each person's life circumstances are influenced. As the positive nature of the teams develops, each person will have deeper personal needs addressed—as expressed by the previous examples.

Action Guides to Practice for Team Synergism

1. *Stay focused on and discuss with others your common goal of creating value for customers.*
2. *Listen to your associates without biases—understand them and what they're saying.*
3. *Look for strengths in each associate and point them out.*
4. *Look for strengths in yourself and point them out to yourself.*
5. *Be thankful each day for the opportunities and livelihood your job provides you.*

As you practice these Action Guides in your everyday life, you'll enjoy the magic of greater influence, appreciation from others, and self-respect for your own skills.

Please remember that if you only read the ideas of this book, and intellectually process them but don't practice them in real-life experiences, you'll profit little. Simply knowing what I write can even cause you to miss the power and magic that only come by application. Most of what I put in these chapters is paradoxical. It often runs counter to our self-focused human natures and is only *emotionally understood* through application in real-life situations.

HOW TO GAIN THE MOST FROM THIS CHAPTER

Your power, effectiveness, energy, and sense of well-being all increase as you're part of a team that functions in a harmonious way toward a common, compelling goal.

You can have several kinds of teams in your life: work teams, recreation teams, spiritual teams, learning teams, family teams, or others that support your goals.

For any team to function most effectively, the following six steps should be followed:

1. *Agree on a goal, vision, or purpose to increase, serve, or create value for customers or other stakeholders.*
2. *Develop a well-defined strategy for attaining the objectives.*
3. *Select the right people who have the appropriate values, work ethics, and customer focus—people who are willing to subordinate their own ego needs to the good of the group.*
4. *Clearly define how each person's job role fits into the team's purpose.*
5. *Measure results and provide for accountability.*
6. *Celebrate and reward performance.*

You may select one or more areas of your life and then put a team together to help you reach goals in that area. You may already be part of a team in your job.

Go back and review the "Relationship Quadrants" illustration. Then rate yourself on the two following self-assessments—"I value you" and "I value me, too." What do you find out? What are your strongest areas? Which ones would you most like to strengthen?

Pick out one trait from "I value you" and one from "I value me, too." Write these on an index card. Read them several times each day, and apply them every chance you have.

Try to review this chapter several times. Practice the Action Guides whenever possible. Look for ways to build up other people, and allow other people to build you up.

Discover the secret of releasing more of your personal energy that comes from being part of a synergistic team.

Applying the concepts of this chapter can propel your career, your personal confidence, and your importance to your organization to new heights.

Self-Assessment: *Practice Teamwork* ✐ ✑

"I Value You"

Take a moment to read each of the following statements. Then circle the number that best describes your actions or thoughts, with *1* being "Never" and *10* being "Always."

1. I look for strengths in you.

   1   2   3   4   5   6   7   8   9   10

2. I see potential in you.

   1   2   3   4   5   6   7   8   9   10

3. I want to understand you.

   1   2   3   4   5   6   7   8   9   10

4. I want you to succeed.

   1   2   3   4   5   6   7   8   9   10

5. I can look past your flaws and focus on your good traits.

   1   2   3   4   5   6   7   8   9   10

6. I want to lift you up.

   1   2   3   4   5   6   7   8   9   10

7. I'm interested in your well-being.

   1   2   3   4   5   6   7   8   9   10

8. I value your ideas.

   1   2   3   4   5   6   7   8   9   10

9. I listen to you.

   1   2   3   4   5   6   7   8   9   10

10. I give you credit when credit is due.

    1   2   3   4   5   6   7   8   9   10

Self-Assessment: *Practice Teamwork* ✎ ✎

"I Value Me, Too!"

Take a moment to read each of the following statements. Then circle the number that best describes your actions or thoughts, with *1* being "Never" and *10* being "Always."

1. I can depend on myself.

    1   2   3   4   5   6   7   8   9   10

2. I keep my commitments.

    1   2   3   4   5   6   7   8   9   10

3. I allow myself to feel good about my achievements.

    1   2   3   4   5   6   7   8   9   10

4. I'm comfortable with my values.

    1   2   3   4   5   6   7   8   9   10

5. I allow my results and actions to speak for themselves.

    1   2   3   4   5   6   7   8   9   10

6. I allow myself to be rewarded when rewards are due.

    1   2   3   4   5   6   7   8   9   10

7. I set goals with a quiet air of confidence that I will reach them.

    1   2   3   4   5   6   7   8   9   10

8. I know that I'll succeed to the extent that I help my team or organization succeed.

    1   2   3   4   5   6   7   8   9   10

9. I measure my own success by the value I create for others.

    1   2   3   4   5   6   7   8   9   10

10. I have a quiet confidence about my abilities because of my strong, positive values.

    1   2   3   4   5   6   7   8   9   10

Action Guide: *Daily Success Diary*

Practice Teamwork

Please score yourself from 1 to 10 for each daily activity, with *1* being "Never" and *10* being "Always."

	S	M	T	W	T	F	S
1. I stayed focused on, and discussed with others, our common goal of creating value for customers.							
2. I listened to my associates without bias.							
3. I looked for strengths in my associates and pointed these strengths out to them.							
4. I looked for strengths in myself and pointed these strengths out to myself.							
5. I was thankful for the opportunity and livelihood my job provides me.							
Total each day							

Service is the pathway to real significance.

(Rick Warren, *The Purpose-Driven Life*)

10 Help Customers

Create Extra Value
for People

As you begin practicing the G. *Val Hi* steps, you'll begin to notice how people with whom you do business or interact either use or fail to use this system. This in itself becomes an unexpected learning experience.

One of our course participants shared the following story of how he learned a lesson about helping people.

> I went to Lowes this past weekend to purchase some home repair stuff. I asked someone where an item was. It clearly wasn't in this person's department, but she took me to it. Then she walked by a bit later to see if I'd found what I was looking for. What impressed me was that this person came out of her department to help me.
>
> Then I went to another department store where I asked a clerk where something was. She sighed and pointed in a general direction. When I asked her to be a bit more specific, she

told me it was not her area and that I'd have to find someone else in that area to help me.

I almost said, "I'm sorry I bothered you." I don't want my customers to feel the way I felt. That experience taught me a lesson.

How many times have you felt that you were bothering a service person when you asked a question or when you just showed up? As you've been learning the G. *Val Hi* system, has your awareness caused you to notice service people's behaviors that you may have previously overlooked? Have your service treatment expectations risen?

So far you've learned these steps in the G. *Val Hi* System:

1. Greet *customers.*
2. Value *customers.*
3. Ask *how to help customers.*
4. Listen *to customers.*

In doing these steps you've done the following:

1. *Caused customers to initially feel welcome and comfortable with you, which has made a great first impression.*
2. *Shown a proper service attitude toward customers by valuing them as people who've blessed your day.*
3. *Asked questions that helped you understand your customers' wants or needs.*
4. *Understood what customers told you and a bit of who they are.*

With these steps completed, it's time to *help* them—to offer solutions to their wants, needs, problems, or objectives.

So let's think about these three Action Guides:

1. *Satisfy customers' wants or needs.*
2. *Solve customers' problems.*
3. *Give customers extra value.*

This chapter is all about taking action. Getting things done. Making customers happy. Solving problems for people. It's the "now that I know what your needs are, here's how I can help you satisfy them" step.

What You Think Your Customers Need . . .

Often what you think your customers' wants or needs are, aren't what *they* perceive them to be. The reason is that people want goods or services not only for what these will do for them, but also for how the goods and services will make them look to others.

While you can't always know people's underlying motivations, you can learn more by careful listening.

Let's look at some examples of how people's needs or wants can be different as they're viewed through the eyes of customers and service people.

Clothing clerk: *That's a size 6 that you want?*

Customer: *What I want is something that will make me look slim for our Christmas party.*

Company tech support person: *I'll be happy to help you understand this new computer program.*

Company associate: *What I really want is to get home on time to attend to my sick child.*

Dentist: *I can give you a pain pill so you will be more comfortable during this procedure.*

Patient: *What I really want is for people to think my teeth are pretty.*

Repairperson: *After we've repaired your watch, it will be as good as new.*

Customer: *I don't know if I really like this watch enough to spend money on it.*

How often do sales or service people assume they know your needs, only to completely miss your real motivations? Could this happen because they don't ask you enough of the right questions?

Satisfy Their Wants or Needs

A customer's desire for certain forms of gratification underlies almost every contact you have with him as you go about your service role. As I've suggested, some needs are obvious, while others lie below the surface. Let's think of *first-level, second-level,* and *third-level* customer needs.

First-level needs *are the obvious ones—"I need to have this problem solved, or want a certain product or service."*

Second-level needs—*"I want to look good and not put myself at risk in this transaction."*

Third-level needs—*"I want to feel that you value me as an important person."*

To summarize these three levels:

Level 1—*to have problems solved or conscious wishes satisfied by products or services*

Level 2—*to minimize risks or look good to others*

Level 3—*to feel good about themselves and value you for the decision or action they took*

To take this further, here are some deeper, sometimes hidden motivations people have that drive their decisions.

- *To be gratified*
- *To feel safe*
- *To feel good about who they are*
- *To be entertained*
- *To receive recognition*
- *To enjoy peace of mind*
- *To "keep up with the Joneses"*
- *To economize or save money*
- *To impress others*
- *To enjoy better health*
- *To acquire or possess*

- *To prevent future loss*
- *To enjoy friendships or have social acceptance*
- *To be accurate or correct*
- *To get ahead in their career*

Depending on the time or other factors that control your contact with customers, you may or may not be able to dig deep enough to understand their Level 2 and 3 motivations. But just knowing that most people have deeper reasons that drive their actions gives you a heads-up if you're aware.

All this works for external customers or internal associates whom you serve or support.

One of our "The Customer" course participants with the American Red Cross wrote about learning this lesson: "Because I deal with collections staff all the time, I have learned to take time to understand what and how they are feeling and do my best to help them any way I can."

To illustrate how important it is to be sensitive to people's feelings, another graduate wrote this: "I had a first-time [blood] donor who was very uncertain as to whether they were going to be able to donate due to nervousness. I spoke with the donor and was very up-front with them as to the vein-puncture procedure and answered all the questions they had. After donating, they came and found me and thanked me for being honest with them and helping them prepare initially for donation. I felt great about putting them at ease."

See the difference between the nurse's need to draw blood and the donor's need to eliminate fear and apprehension?

It's easy for service people to stay so fixed on their need to achieve their own goals that they don't put themselves in their customers' shoes and truly understand their needs. They're often worlds apart.

Again, almost all the people we serve or work with have special needs that we can help them fill or satisfy. They may perceive a situation totally differently than we do. When you see your job or relationship with others as helping them fill their needs or wants, your questions and subsequent actions will be influenced.

Douglas Smith, a community developer of Bloomfield, Michigan, summed the point up well when he wrote:

> In my position, I regularly deal with people who, because of our development within a community, fear that they will be adversely affected. In many cases, our relationships are initially wrought with animosity and distrust, and frankly, it was a stretch to believe that these, too, were my customers.
>
> However, through constant use of the *Greet, Value, Ask, Listen, Help, Invite System,* and a better understanding of how these folks, if asked, can become your greatest advocates, now I am enjoying greater success working with them.

Let me emphasize that simply acquiring your product or service isn't what customers want—they want to fill a deeper need. Said another way, what you provide them isn't their need—their need is for the reward or gratification that your product or service will help them enjoy.

Understand this and you'll clearly see how you and your customers can be on different motivational pages. Your focus is to deliver a product or service; theirs is to enjoy an end-result benefit.

Solve Their Problems

In Chapter 5 you learned a problem-solving formula. It gave you a step-by-step process:

1. Understand *the problem.*
2. Identify *the cause.*
3. Discuss *possible solutions.*
4. Solve *the problem.*

I stressed that effective problem solving is more than knowing a process; rather, it's having a problem-solving *mind-set*. It's defining what you do in the following ways:

- *"I'm here to help internal and external customers solve their problems."*
- *"The more problems they have, the more I can help them."*
- *"The more I help solve people's problems, the more successful I'll be."*
- *"I view people's problems as opportunities for me."*
- *"I welcome people's problems as ways to do my job more effectively."*
- *"Solving larger problems is the price of my ticket to higher compensation, respect of others, and personal satisfaction."*

Want to do an experiment that can boost your self-confidence when facing customers' problems? Try this:

1. *Write the six previous self-suggestions on an index card or enter them in your daily planner.*
2. *Read them to yourself several times each day.*
3. *Each time you read them, take one minute to silently repeat them to yourself several times. Each time, visualize what they mean.*

The repetition of this exercise over a period of time will begin to create new beliefs in your "I Am" dimension. As this begins to happen, you'll feel more and more confidence in your abilities. You'll view problems differently, and this will unconsciously motivate and energize you. You'll gradually welcome problems as positive opportunities, rather than thorny issues that you'd rather avoid.

Create a New Problem-Solving Paradigm

Each of us views problems differently. Our unconscious beliefs about our ability to solve certain problems influences the ones we attempt to solve. We frustrate and stress ourselves if we only intellectually learn the problem-solving formula and don't actually practice it. Until our unconscious values, self-beliefs, and views of our own possibilities change, our ability to face and solve problems will stay pretty much the same.

OUR UNCONSCIOUS PROBLEM-SOLVING PARADIGM

Weak	*Strong*
Self-focused	Other-focused
Avoidance-oriented	Action-oriented
Ego-involved	Fact-based
Fear-focused	Solutions-focused
Defensive	Open

Each of us has our own *problem-solving paradigm,* or our individual frame of reference. This mental and emotional boundary defines:

1. *The abilities we think we have to solve problems.*

2. *The size problems we believe we can solve.*

3. *The rewards we unconsciously believe we deserve to have.*

This unconscious problem-solving paradigm has been developed by your responses to your life experiences. It's only changed *experientially,* not *intellectually.* To be honest, you'll not solve larger problems until this unconscious paradigm expands. Said another way, by reading this book you'll only gain knowledge, but you will not influence your ability to solve larger problems until you *practice* the advice I give you and grow new habits.

Your internal view of your own possibilities expands only as you take action, practice the ideas I share with you, and enjoy successful outcomes. Your self-beliefs are expanded only as you structure daily successes. Successes prepare you for more successes.

Start Where You Are . . .

My advice is to begin where you are now by tackling problems that are just a bit beyond your current challenges. Don't jump from your present problem levels to ones six steps higher. Make several incremental steps, as shown in the model below, "Increases in Problem Size." This way you'll build success upon success on a daily basis.

Clearly understand the level of problems you currently solve. Define ones that are just a bit higher. As in the model, jump to 1; don't immediately try to go to 3.

The world is full of people, in all kinds of professions, who got in "over their heads," stumbled, and never were emotionally able to pick themselves up again.

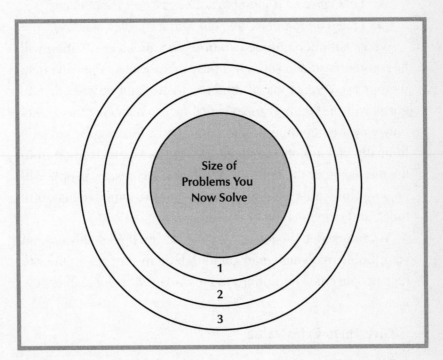

Increases in Problem Size

Carefully expand your problem-solving ability in a step-by-step manner.

Have a Problem-Solving Attitude

I've written a lot about how we individually view problems. But let's get right down to a core issue: *What mind-set do you bring with you to problems?*

Here are some different self-views that I've experienced.

- *"I greet this as an opportunity to create value for this person."*
- *"Every problem has a logical solution."*
- *"It's all about arriving at a win-win solution."*
- *"I have no agenda but to work with you to reach a satisfactory solution."*
- *"Let's agree on a solution, not haggle over the problem."*
- *"I focus on solutions, and don't attack people's motives."*

Whatever inner attitude you bring to a problem situation will be communicated to your customers or associates. You can't help it. Your eye contact, facial muscles, hands, and other body language will tip them off to your real focus. Whatever this is, not only will it be communicated consciously, but people will subliminally pick up on your feelings. And as you've learned from the discussion of the *law of psychological reciprocity*, people will be powerfully motivated to return to you the same feelings, attitudes, and emotions you give to them.

As you practice the ideas in this book, you'll gradually expand your problem-solving paradigm and develop stronger abilities to help people enjoy resolutions to their many different challenges.

Give Them Extra Value

The third Action Guide to *help* customers is this: *Give them extra value.*

I've written much about this mind-set. Really, the whole book is focused on this one objective. In a very real sense, your *commercial value* is determined by the value you give others above what they expect to receive.

For a moment let's think of an interesting word, "lagniappe" (pronounced "LAN-yap"). A lagniappe is a small, unexpected gift.

After a delicious meal, when your coffee is served and the waiter surprises you with a tray of assorted chocolates, he's giving you a lagniappe. Or after you've signed the papers for your new car, when the salesperson walks you to a room filled with coffee mugs, key rings, watches, jackets, and other items and asks you to pick out one, that gift is a lagniappe. After you help an associate with a project, if he or she sends you a nice *thank-you* note, that's a lagniappe.

Lagniappe is anything extra that, after you've completed a transaction in a satisfactory manner, you give a customer. It's the icing on the cake—when the customer consciously or unconsciously says to you "I'm completely satisfied with your service, solution, or help," you then give that person a little extra value.

There are many forms of extra value. You'll have your own unique ones, depending on the person or occasion.

How can you give *something extra* in an everyday way on your job? Here's how some of our course graduates reported doing it.

- *"A customer told me that he just received word that his wife had cancer. I took extra time to listen to him and help him feel better."*
- *"An angry employee was calmed down when I used the skills I learned in this course to actively listen. She did not resign and seemed to be much happier after our talk that day."*
- *"I try to always call customers back after solving a problem or helping them. Then I write a note to them, thanking them for their loyalty. Each time I do this, I feel better about me and my job."*

Lagniappe is most effective when it's unexpected.

After remodeling my home, I sold it and moved to a condominium in a high-rise building. I gave most of my furniture away and bought all new things. I went to a table linens and gift shop and bought more than $2,000 worth of things. Remembering that when I was in that business, and people bought items from me, I always gave them something extra, I blurted out, almost without thinking, "How about throwing in some nice candles?"

The clerk looked at me with a stunned expression and then had to go ask the owner, who came out, looked at me, and said, "We don't usually do that!"

I suddenly felt awkward for even asking.

Reluctantly, the owner wrapped up a couple of candles and handed them to me, gave me a stare that said "This really pains me," and walked away. She didn't say "Thank you" or anything.

Her actions caused me to feel a little cheap even for asking, along with feeling unappreciated. The clerk was very nice and appreciative, but it didn't excuse the owner's response.

Hey, I know what kind of markup they have on gift items, and . . . the two candles couldn't have cost them more than $10.

Contrast that with how Susan Davis of the Kreiss Collection used the *lagniappe* idea. After buying furniture from her, I received several phone calls to see if everything was okay. She sent a touch-up person by just to check on any nicks that may have happened in delivery. She came by my home after each delivery to check on how everything looked. She called me one day and volunteered to redo a chair cushion so it would look better. She went out of her way to shop for accessory pieces—from which she made no income.

Sure, the furniture cost more than the gift items did, but it was the different attitude that stood out.

Dave Orman is my barber. He tells me that 85 percent of his clients have been with him over five years. For me, a haircut is a haircut is a haircut. The volume of my hair doesn't leave barbers opportunity for a lot of creativity. In fact, Dave takes a seven-minute job and stretches it to fifteen.

Three times he's come to my home to give me a haircut after I've had surgery. He makes the experience fun. He gives me really "bad" speaking material (which I wouldn't dare use with a paying audience). Here's one of his best bad jokes (you don't want to even hear any of the worst bad ones): "Did you hear about the skeleton who went into a bar and ordered a beer and a mop?"

Okay, pick yourself up off the floor.

I can be all stressed out because of some business challenge, or other problems, and go to Dave. Without exception, he makes my time with him fun, taking my mind off business or whatever. He has a special gift of adding joy to his clients' days.

He turns a haircut into a pleasant experience, giving *something extra*—himself.

Lagniappe.

My daughter, Robin, who lives in Dallas, raves about the value-added service she receives at Bibbentucker's, an upscale dry cleaner.

This business is at a busy corner in north Dallas and has a circle drive that enters from one street and exits on another. When Robin drives through under a large awning, immediately a sharply dressed associate runs to her car, asks for her name, and relates it to the personnel inside. At this point, the magic of value-added occurs: This associate offers her a choice of iced tea or lemonade in summer, or coffee in winter. They even have a large fishbowl full of dog treats for customers who bring their furry friends.

Robin says the amazing thing is that, if a customer has a drop-off, the employees remember that person's name if the person has been there previously.

On more than one occasion, she has had laundry in her backseat, intending to go to a less expensive cleaners, yet she took it to Bibbentucker's for the cold glass of iced tea.

Can You Measure Your Extra Value?

Can you quantify the extra value you give your customers or associates? When you satisfy their wants or needs, or solve their problems, what extra value can you give them that they don't expect?

Do you help people feel better about themselves and their service experiences? Do you give them a part of yourself—your expertise, experience, knowledge, or friendship? Can you measure the impact of these gifts?

"Difficult," you say? Of course. But here's my point. Always try to place a measurement on how your extra value helps them. Just thinking about it will help reinforce the habit. When you do it—and here's the most important part of giving extra value—keep it a secret. Don't broadcast your good deeds. Let your customers do that—if it's done. Remind yourself that your highest reward is simply knowing what you've done. As the philosopher Henry Drummond put it, "After you've done the good deed, put a seal on your lips, and forget what you have done."

True confidence and wholesome self-esteem happen to the extent that you silently stack up your extra-mile actions. When only *you* know what you've done, your bank account of self-respect will grow and grow.

There are so many compensations to the person who gives extra value to others simply for the personal joy of doing it.

1. *It provides the only logical reason to expect greater compensation.*
2. *It builds your self-esteem as nothing else can.*
3. *It builds the confidence of others in your integrity.*
4. *It forms the foundation for continued personal growth.*

5. *It brings you to the attention of your managers.*

6. *It eliminates your competition from winning your customers.*

Unfortunately, today there are too many people whose attitude is "Give me more pay for less work!" This prevalent thinking kills initiative and leads to mediocrity and the stagnation of willpower and success consciousness.

If you truly desire to enjoy greater career, personal, and relationship success, you have no better guide than rendering more and better service than that for which you're paid. This paradoxical practice in time turns all your efforts into personal prosperity.

We can ignore this natural law of increasing returns, but we can't escape its consequences.

HOW TO GAIN THE MOST FROM THIS CHAPTER

Please carefully read this chapter and see if what I write about is congruent with your inner beliefs and values.

Do you believe that your success is determined by the value you create for people? By the degree to which you *help* them? Is your focus not just to do your job, deal with customers, or even solve their problems, but to create value for them as a *result*?

Please study these customer motivations.

First-level needs—*"I need to have this problem solved, or a certain product or service."*

Second-level needs—*"I want to look good and not put myself at risk in this transaction."*

Third-level needs—*"I want to feel that you value me as an important person."*

Review the six self-suggestions that can reveal your mind-set about problem solving.

- *"I'm here to help internal and external customers solve their problems."*

- *"The more problems they have, the more I can help them."*
- *"The more I help solve people's problems, the more successful I'll be."*
- *"I view people's problems as opportunities for me."*
- *"I welcome people's problems as ways to do my job more effectively."*
- *"Solving larger problems is the price of my ticket to higher compensation, respect of others, and personal satisfaction."*

Try writing these self-suggestions on an index card, or other places where you'll see them frequently. Read and repeat them several times each day. Doing this, over a period of time, will help program them into the deep beliefs in your "I Am" dimension.

Create a new problem-solving paradigm. Identify the size of problems you're currently solving. Then commit yourself to ones that are just a bit beyond your current abilities. Get good at solving larger problems, build your confidence, and then select even higher ones. Remember, you grow increment by increment, not in giant leaps.

Each time you have contact with people, select a way to give extra value to them. Often, simple ways are the most memorable.

Remember the word "lagniappe," or *something extra*.

Make an effort to practice giving extra value daily.

Self-Assessment: *Help Customers*

Take a moment to read each of the following statements. Then circle the number that best describes your actions or thoughts, with *1* being "Never" and *10* being "Always."

1. My main purpose in working with people is to help create value for them.

   1   2   3   4   5   6   7   8   9   10

2. Before I offer solutions to people, I first thoroughly understand their needs.

   1   2   3   4   5   6   7   8   9   10

3. In helping customers, I look for deeper motivations than their need for my product or service.

   1   2   3   4   5   6   7   8   9   10

4. I welcome customers' problems as opportunities.

   1   2   3   4   5   6   7   8   9   10

5. I constantly look for larger problems to solve.

   1   2   3   4   5   6   7   8   9   10

6. I keep my own ego and defensiveness out of customer conflicts.

   1   2   3   4   5   6   7   8   9   10

7. I constantly look for ways to give customers or associates extra value.

   1   2   3   4   5   6   7   8   9   10

8. I look for ways to measure the impact of my extra value.

   1   2   3   4   5   6   7   8   9   10

9. I have no need to broadcast my good deeds.

   1   2   3   4   5   6   7   8   9   10

10. I believe my personal success and self-esteem are tied to the value I give others.

   1   2   3   4   5   6   7   8   9   10

Action Guide: *Daily Success Diary*

Help Customers

Please score yourself from 1 to 10 for each daily activity, with
1 being "Never" and *10* being "Always."

	S	M	T	W	T	F	S
1. I focused on satisfying a customer's wants and needs.							
2. I helped solve a person's problem.							
3. I gave extra value to each person today.							
4. I gave extra value and kept it a secret.							
5. I learned from people with whom I do business.							
Total each day							

Every living creature has a built-in guidance system or goal-seeking device, put there by its Creator to help it achieve its goal.

(Dr. Maxwell Maltz)

11 Set Goals

Expand Your Future Success and Fulfillment

"Just think, it all started when I attended your seminar," the young man ended his note to me, after explaining that he'd just been accepted into medical school.

Reading this, my mind floated back a few years to when I was conducting a goal-achievement seminar in Dallas. A friend, Norman Pahmeier, brought his son Gene kicking and screaming to my first evening session. Gene was nineteen or twenty years old, very clean-cut and bright-looking. His father told me that he'd just been lying around the house—not knowing what he wanted to do. He'd gone to Texas A & M University for two years and then dropped out.

When the second evening session finished, Gene came up to me and asked some questions. I could tell something had rung a bell in his mind. He'd sat in the front row and taken lots of notes.

His father called a few days later and said, "Boy, you really got

Gene fired up! He's set a goal to go back to college and become a physical therapist."

Gene soon entered a university and completed physical therapy school with honors—having a 3.5 grade-point average. He went on to graduate from medical school with honors. After that, he sent me another note of thanks.

Today Gene Pahmeier, M.D., is a medical and surgical ophthalmologist in private practice in Alabama. After physical therapy school, he entered the U.S. Army Reserve and went through medical school. He then joined the Army to do his residency. Later he became a flight surgeon, and one year was honored as the Flight Surgeon of the Year in the whole U.S. Army.

What triggered this series of events?

Discover Your Inner Goal-Seeking Mechanism

Gene Pahmeier discovered and activated his goal-seeking mechanism. He was at a crossroads in his life, and the events of the seminar triggered something within him to take action.

You and I possess this same inner mechanism. You've always had it. Everyone does. Most people, however, never discover it or have the motivation to activate it. So it lies dormant—unused and inactive.

This mechanism is a part of your brain and nervous system put there by your Creator to help you live a productive life.

Here's how it works.

1. *You select a goal.*
2. *You visualize its reality.*
3. *You savor its rewards.*
4. *You consciously and unconsciously evaluate the possibility of it actually happening.*
5. *You, both consciously and unconsciously, determine your worthiness of receiving the rewards of reaching the goal.*

At this point something happens within you. If your responses to these five thought processes are positive, your automatic goal-seeking mechanism is immediately activated and goes to work to steer you to the goal. But if your responses are doubtful or negative, your inner mechanism stays inactive.

When this powerful inner mechanism is activated, through desire and belief it begins to silently steer you to your goals. We all use this in everyday ways like driving to work, solving a simple problem, or remembering someone's name, but we are blinded to its availability for more important goals.

Here's an ordinary way to understand the power of this inner mechanism. Pick out your favorite comfort food—mixed nuts, popcorn, pecan praline ice cream, peanut butter and Ritz crackers, whatever you have a difficult time avoiding if it's available to you. If you don't have it in your pantry or refrigerator now, go buy it.

Wait until around nine one evening and, while you're relaxing, consciously visualize how it would taste. Think back to the last time you experienced the taste; then just allow your senses to explore how wonderful it would be.

Do this for a few minutes and see what inner urge moves you out of your chair and into the kitchen.

Then analyze what happened.

1. *You pictured a goal.*
2. *You visualized the rewards of having that goal.*
3. *You knew it was available.*
4. *Your desire level overpowered your knowledge that calories count.*
5. *You were emotionally guided to the goal.*

Like this simple experiment, when you have a goal that seems available, and you emotionalize your desire for it, something within you takes over and guides you to it.

In his classic book *Psycho-Cybernetics*, Dr. Maxwell Maltz makes these observations about this mechanism.

1. *Your built-in mechanism must have a goal or target.*
2. *This target must be conceived of as* already *in existence now, either in actual or potential form.*
3. *The mechanism operates either by*
    a. *steering you to a goal already in existence or*
    b. *discovering the elements to put together to form something that hasn't previously existed.*

Unleashing the power of your automatic goal-seeking mechanism doesn't demand logic or willpower; rather, it's released by your imagination and belief. Actually, everyday logic can often block the attainment of your goals—especially the *logic* of negative people around you who love to tell you "It can't be done."

I'll give you all the steps you need to know to activate your own success mechanism in this chapter. It'll be up to you to take action, if you're motivated to achieve higher goals.

But before we go on, let me ask, "What is that *magic something* that motivates one person to higher achievements, while others choose to stay where they are?"

Let's think of it.

Inspirational Dissatisfaction

The main motivator of personal growth and achievement is the *desire* to have, gain, or possess something that you do not now enjoy.

Basically, you're motivated by either (or both) of these two factors:

- *The hope of gain.*
- *The fear of pain.*

Inspirational dissatisfaction is being thankful for what you have and where you are, but at the same time feeling a stewardship obligation to be all that you can be. It's here that your motive for growth can be healthy or unhealthy.

The desire to grow, develop, and achieve more, when motivated by a genuine desire to give back and create value, ennobles you and brings true satisfaction. But if your motivation is fueled by the desire to keep, store up, and serve only yourself, paradoxically, you'll miss much of the joy and happiness that you otherwise could have experienced. True satisfaction can easily elude you.

To what extent do you have *inspirational dissatisfaction?* How strongly do you want to:

1. *learn more than you now know?*
2. *contribute more to your organization?*
3. *give more value to your internal or external customers?*
4. *create a better life for your family?*
5. *enjoy things that you aren't now enjoying?*
6. *earn more than you are now earning?*
7. *improve your health or wellness?*
8. *deepen your spiritual discernment?*
9. *enjoy greater financial security?*
10. *contribute more to the welfare of others?*

How you answer the questions determines your true level of desire, or *inspirational dissatisfaction.* The intensity of your *desire level* will then predict your success in reaching higher goals.

Today . . . A Great Time to Begin

Would you please stop reading for a few moments and go back and read the ten questions I just asked. Carefully think about them. Do they create any *inspirational dissatisfaction* in you? Do they cause discomfort within you? Do they cause you to call up feelings of zest, enthusiasm, or hope? Or do they cause you to dig up feelings of past failure, despair, or hopelessness? Or a mixture of both?

Today . . . now . . . this moment is a great time to decide to move ahead and bury past limiting feelings. You don't have to stay stuck. Whatever your past is, you can decide right now to advance in the direction of your dreams, access real capabilities, or reach your true possibilities. You can, by adding nothing to your present life except a *genuine desire* to be, have, or contribute more.

If you truly have this *inspirational dissatisfaction*, then you'll recognize what I'll share with you in the rest of this chapter.

So, let's go deeper.

Goal Achievement—An Internal Issue

You don't reach goals just by writing them down. All of us have set goals that never happened. Deeper dimensions within us are responsible for their actual attainment.

Notice the "Goal-Achievement Congruence Model," shown below.

Five dimensions—goal clarity, view of possibilities, values, achievement drive, and supportive environment—must come into congruence for your goals to happen. Let me emphasize that

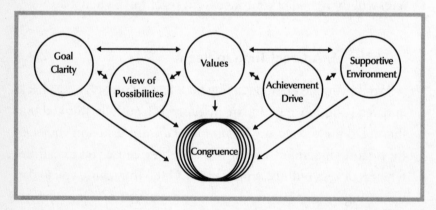

Goal-Achievement Congruence Model

bringing them into congruence is a developmental process, not an intellectual one. Unconscious processes, not conscious, logical ones, make goals happen. Conflicts block them. Here are some examples of conflicts between these five dimensions.

- *Setting goals but not unconsciously believing them to be possible.*
- *Setting goals that are in conflict with your values.*
- *Setting goals but not having sufficient desire or drive to make them happen.*
- *Setting goals but having people, places, or things that torpedo them.*

Let me define each of these dimensions in a bit more detail.

GOAL CLARITY

Goal clarity is having clear statements that describe desirable future events in your life. These statements must be specific, quantifiable, and clear of generalities like the words "more," "better," "good," "some," "increased," and so on. You'll also need to have specific target dates for their achievement.

Your goal statements should be statements of the desired end-results—what you want to end up happening. Here are some general examples of goal statements.

- *Beginning July 1, I will work out four days each week at the gym.*
- *By November 15, I'll finish my course in graphic design.*
- *By April 1, I'll reduce customer complaints by 20 percent.*
- *By January 15, I'll be proficient in our new accounting system.*
- *On June 10, my family will enjoy a trip to Disneyland.*

See how these statements are specific and have target dates? Later in this chapter, I'll ask you to take time out to write your own goals.

View of Possibilities

View of possibilities refers to your unconscious beliefs about what goals are possible for you to reach. All of us have our own, unique *area-of-the-possible*. This consists of our accumulated beliefs about what we're *capable* of achieving and what rewards we *deserve* to enjoy. This internal boundary either allows new goals to happen or blocks them.

Look at the illustration below, "The Possible and the Impossible." Let the inner circle represent your *area-of-the-possible*, and the outer one signify your *area-of-the-impossible*.

Whatever your *area-of-the-possible* is, it contains and controls all your

- *actions,*
- *feelings,*
- *behavior,* and
- *abilities.*

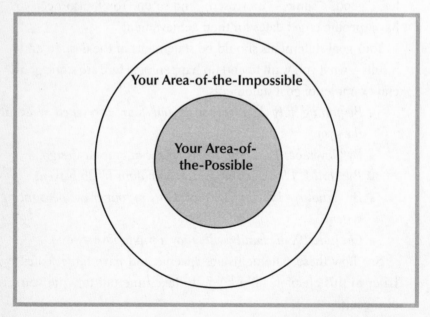

The Possible and the Impossible

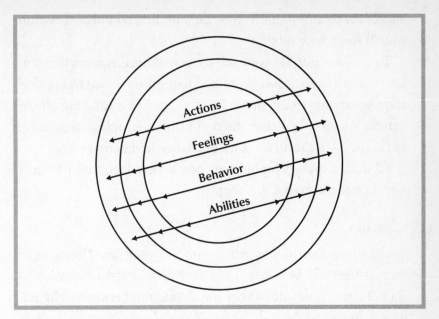

Expanding the Possible

Now look at "Expanding the Possible," above. This model shows that your actions, feelings, behavior, and abilities only expand as your internal *area-of-the-possible* gets larger.

Let me emphasize that your current *area-of-the-possible* isn't the result of knowledge, logic, or reality. It's the result of your *perception* of reality. It's the result of unconscious pictures or images you hold as truth. But they're not always actual truth! The reality is that you have the potential for unlimited achievement. But to realize that potential, your inner beliefs must first change. To change your reality, you must first change certain unconscious images and self-perceptions.

All this programming is taking place in your "I Am" dimension. Your *area-of-the-possible* has been developed by your responses to your life experiences. This emotional and spiritual boundary acts as a barrier to keep you from performing beyond it. In simple terms: You will rarely reach goals that are outside your *area-of-the-possible*—until you expand the boundaries within your "I Am" dimension.

To perform outside your self-set boundaries requires that you focus your inner goal-seeking mechanism on new targets, and allow it to guide you to them. You first have to break through old beliefs, which may cause discomfort or even initial resistance. Let's face it—we're all resistant to change in different ways.

I'll share a strategy for building new beliefs deep within your "I Am" before the end of this chapter.

VALUES

Values are the rules by which you live your life. They govern your actions and behavior. They're at the deepest foundation of your "I Am." Your values help you distinguish between right and wrong. As you go through life, you're constantly unconsciously or consciously defining your values. When faced with problems or difficulties, you'll answer the following questions with your actions, and as you do, your values will be automatically demonstrated.

- *How will I handle this problem?*
- *Will I tell the truth when a half-truth might get me over the hump?*
- *Will I present my product or service claims correctly?*
- *Will I make the calls, contacts, or follow-up activities that I commit to making?*
- *Will I focus on how much I can get or how much I can give?*
- *Will I take shortcuts, or will I build solid foundations for long-term success?*
- *Will I take responsibility for my actions, or will I blame others?*
- *Will I be open to learn from others, even those who criticize me?*
- *Will I look for my life's purpose?*
- *Will I view problems and personal weaknesses as learning aids?*

To the extent that your conscious choices are congruent with your unconscious beliefs or values, you'll enjoy emotional strength.

ACHIEVEMENT DRIVE

Achievement drive is a latent, potential power that everyone possesses. It usually stays dormant, because most people lack goal clarity. But once you have clear goals that you passionately desire to reach, deeply believe to be within your possibilities, and feel worthy of achieving, you automatically release this energy according to the intensity of your inner beliefs and desires.

Achievement drive causes persistence, a dogged determination, and a never-give-up attitude. It drives you to learn what you must know to be successful, and then motivates you to develop the necessary skills to reach higher goals.

SUPPORTIVE ENVIRONMENT

Supportive environment is having people, places, or things around you that assist you in reaching your goals.

We all need a few people who will encourage us and support us to reach higher goals. Unfortunately, many of us have people in our lives who don't want us to reach higher goals. These are people who might be threatened by our new levels of success. Or they may be highly resistant to changes and not want you to change, either. Or they may be controlling people who would feel a loss of power if you changed.

On a positive side, we all need one or two people with whom we can share our goals, knowing that they'll support us, help us, and be delighted when we succeed. My caution to you is not to reveal your goals to anyone who'll react negatively, or in any way try to block you. Guard your goals as you'd guard your life savings.

Enjoying Goal Clarity

Using the worksheet that follows, please take an hour or so to define some goals in different areas of your life (for example, skills that you want to acquire), and then answer the question "What do I want to happen in this general area of my life?"

MY CAREER OR WORK?

_____

- Skills?

_____

- Position?

_____

- Service level?

_____

- Results?

_____

- Other?

_____

MY PERSONAL LIFE?

_____

- Weight?

_____

- Education?

_____

- Recreation?

_____

- Health and fitness?

_____

- Other?

_____

MY FAMILY LIFE?

- Relationships?

- Activities?

- Projects?

- Home?

- Other?

MY FINANCIAL LIFE?

- Income?

- Savings?

- Retirement?

- Investments?

- Other?

MY SPIRITUAL LIFE?

- Growth and learning?

- Core beliefs?

- Study time?

- Prayer time?

_____

- Other?

_____

MY SOCIAL LIFE?

_____

- Activities?

_____

- Type of acquaintances?

_____

- Places to go?

_____

- Skills needed?

_____

- Other?

_____

As you review these six goal categories and the suggested areas under each one, focus on one or two goals that are most meaningful to you.

When you've identified your goals, please take out index cards and write each goal on a separate card. Then put a paper clip or rubber band around the deck of cards. Keep your goal cards handy so you can read and review them several times daily.

Then, by doing the following activities, you'll begin to program your goal-seeking mechanism to lead you to your desired objectives.

Expanding Your View of Your Possibilities

When it's sufficiently programmed and allowed to function, your inner goal-seeking mechanism will automatically lead you to successful achievement.

Your goal-seeking mechanism was imbedded into your "I Am" when you came into the world. As I've mentioned before, it remains dormant for most people—undiscovered and unused, never able to lead them to their desired goals. The more you discover and access this powerful inner mechanism, the more you'll expand your unconscious view of your possibilities. Moreover, the more you enlarge your *area-of-the-possible*, the more your goal-seeking mechanism will work for you.

Here are some actions, or activities, you can take to make these happen.

1. *Find one or two people who are achieving goals you'd like to enjoy. Study them—what they do, what they read, where they go, with whom they associate, and from whom they learn.*

   a. *Ask if you can learn from them. Perhaps invite them out for lunch or breakfast. Ask how they got to where they are today. Be a learner—listen.*

   b. *Extract specific success principles to practice. Commit yourself to applying them. Report back on your success with their ideas.*

2. *Select rewards you'll give yourself when you reach specific goals. Realize that we work only for the promise of rewards. This is the essence of self-motivation.*

   a. *First, you must identify rewards, then feast your mind on them daily. Visualize yourself already enjoying them. Get pictures of them to look at each day. Think and talk to yourself as if you already had them.*

   b. *Keep your goals a secret from all but one or two positive people, until you actually reach them. Your talking about them can drain your desire and energy. Also, you'll probably encounter people who'll try to discourage you before you have the rewards. Discouragement can be deadly.*

3. *Feast your eyes on beauty and good design.*

   a. *Study beautiful landscapes, homes, art, products—whatever is right for you, and wherever you find it. Don't go to buy, but simply to observe and absorb. Turn your emotions loose and allow them to enjoy the beauty of what you see.*

b. *Read classic wisdom literature—perhaps Emerson's essays, Benjamin Franklin's autobiography, the Bible, especially Psalms, Proverbs, and Ecclesiastes, or whatever else is most meaningful for you.*

4. *Recall past success.*

a. *Enjoy the memories of success.*

b. *Play the "If I could then, I can now" game. Tell yourself if you could reach a past goal, you can also reach higher goals now.*

Your gradual observance of these success strategies will expand your internal *view of possibilities.*

Developing Values

Select a few timeless values and stick by them—even when it's tempting to stray. Here are a few that will serve your long-term success well:

- *I do the right thing, because it's the right thing to do.*
- *I tell the truth unless it would hurt someone.*
- *When I make a commitment, I keep it.*
- *I listen to people without biases.*
- *When I see something that needs to be done, I do it.*
- *I succeed by helping others succeed.*

Develop your own personal set of values. Repeat them to yourself often. Let them guide your decisions and actions.

Releasing Achievement Drive

Achievement drive is released from within you as your unconscious views of your possibilities increase. Your own belief that your goals are possible causes this energy to be released from within you. This power then causes persistence and determination that will carry you through the road blocks, occasional discouragement, and other difficulties we all face.

Here are some suggestions to help you increase your desire level, or achievement drive.

Form a *growth group* of two or three other people who share your desire to enjoy higher career or personal goals. Meet once a week for an hour. Each of you should read the same self-help book or listen to a recorded message.

Some of my favorite self-help classes are

- *Psycho-Cybernetics*, by Maxwell Maltz, M.D.
- *Think and Grow Rich*, by Napoleon Hill
- *The Magic of Believing*, by Claude Bristol

Some excellent newer books are

- *The 7 Habits of Highly Successful People*, by Stephen Covey
- *Emotional Intelligence*, by Daniel Goleman
- *Wisdom of the Ages*, by Wayne Dyer

1. *In your hour have each participant share*
   a. *a success principle he or she practiced;*
   b. *how he or she applied the principle;*
   c. *what happened, or what his or her results were.*
2. *After each participant shares his or her story, the rest of the group spends a couple of minutes mentioning specific points they learned from the person's experience and praises the person's results.*
3. *Spend the balance of the hour pointing out strengths in each other and talking about the application of the success principles that were shared.*

These sessions must be conducted in a totally positive environment. Do not allow negative talk to enter in. Do not talk critically of other people. Negativism will destroy the success of your meetings. In time this association of positive people—all dedicated to helping each other become more successful—will help you enjoy tremendous growth.

For more ideas, study in *The Autobiography of Benjamin Franklin* the *Junta* (group) he established and credits with much of his great success. Or read Napoleon Hill's classic *Think and Grow Rich,* and study his Master Mind concept.

Structure a Supportive Environment

A *supportive environment* will be partially developed with the growth group concept I've just described. In addition, you'll want to give special attention to four levels of relationships you need in order to function with optimum courage and minimum emotional clutter. Carefully think of these.

Level 1—*A very intimate, nonjudgmental relationship with one or two people with whom you can be totally open and feel totally accepted. In this kind of relationship, you feel no need to wear masks.*

Level 2—*An intimate, nonjudgmental relationship with three to five people wherein each gives and receives unconditional support. This can be with miscellaneous friends or people with whom you work. It can also be you, your spouse, and another couple. Like Level 1 relationships, this level offers total acceptance of each other. In both Level 1 and Level 2 relationships, people accept each other for their value as persons. Acceptance is not based on actions.*

Level 3—*A friendly relationship with eight to twelve people: a study group, a sales group, or other meetings of people with common interests. This group can have meaningful interaction, though less intense or intimate.*

Level 4—*A relationship that results from belonging to a larger group wherein you receive less intense support or fellowship.*

> *This can be a civic club, luncheon group, professional associ-*
> *ation, church, or other larger group that gives you enjoyment*
> *and a sense of belonging, and in which you have many ac-*
> *quaintances.*

These support groups help you enjoy healthy relationships with people with whom you have common beliefs and values.

Desire, Not Willpower, Leads to Goals

Goals aren't achieved by sheer *willpower* as much as by building your conscious and unconscious desires for the *rewards* that reaching goals will help you enjoy.

Your mind is so complex that it encompasses both the conscious and unconscious parts of you. With your conscious "I Think" mind, you use logic, learn, and think. But the unconscious "I Am" part of you is the dynamic, creative part that directs you to your goals. Your goal-seeking mechanism goes to work to bring into reality the goals your conscious mind sets—when they're congruent with your inner beliefs, values, and environmental influences.

You can observe this in many of your daily activities. Have you ever been preoccupied and lost in thought while driving to work? You got to work, but you didn't consciously notice a thing along the way? What happened was, knowing your goal, your unconscious mechanism directed you until it was reached. Now, this may not sound too profound, but when you experience it and then analyze it, it's almost miraculous.

Another way to observe your unconscious silently at work is through your hunches and intuition. Ever wrestle with a problem to no avail, only to wake up at 3:00 A.M. with the solution clearly in focus? This happens all the time—because your inner guidance systems are silently at work within you, steering you to your goal, the answer to your problem.

When you begin to learn this concept, you'll see how your unconscious goal-seeking mechanism works in many ways. You'll then be excited to know that you can direct it and let it help you reach any goal that's important to you.

As this happens, you will gain tremendous personal power.

HOW TO GAIN THE MOST FROM THIS CHAPTER

Many people who set goals fail to reach them. This begs the question "Why?"

Goal achievement is an internal belief issue, not an external willpower one. You have an unconscious goal-seeking mechanism that can help you enjoy important goals—when you learn to program it and allow it to guide you to your targets.

It all begins with *inspirational dissatisfaction.* This is a state of being thankful for what you have and where you are, but at the same time feeling a stewardship to be all that you can be.

Please go back and meditate on the ten questions I asked you near the beginning of this chapter. As you honestly answer them, you'll get an idea of your level of desire.

Remember that goal achievement is an issue of developing an inner congruence of these factors.

1. *Goal clarity*
2. *View of possibilities*
3. *Values*
4. *Achievement drive*
5. *Supportive environment*

Carefully think of times when you reached goals, or failed to attain them, and see if you can identify the congruence, or lack of it, in these five dimensions.

Where conflicts between the five factors exist, goal achievement will be hampered. By following my suggestions, you'll gradually eliminate conflicts and bring your goals into congruence. This will give you personal and emotional power.

Please take some time to set goals in any or all of these six areas:

- *Career or work*
- *Personal life*
- *Family life*
- *Financial life*
- *Spiritual life*
- *Social life*

Be sure to state them as I've suggested, putting a target or beginning date on them. You'll be amazed at how effective it is to print your statements on index cards and refer to them several times each day.

Remember to set your goals just a bit beyond your current level of achievement. This will cause you to receive quicker gratification and reach them sooner. Then as soon as you reach a goal, set another one just a bit higher, and continue to repeat this process.

Be satisfied with incremental growth, and know that in no time at all, you'll look back and notice you've made exciting gains.

Set up a growth group. Study successful people. Learn from them. Go where they go. Do what they do. Learn what they learn.

From time to time you'll find it beneficial to come back to this chapter and carefully perform all the activities I shared with you. As you do, you'll discover ideas and success principles you didn't see before.

You'll discover that successful living is a continuing process, not a destination. You'll marvel that the more you discover about your true potential, greater and greater possibilities will be opened up to you.

Self-Assessment: *Set Goals* ✏️ ✎

Take a moment to read each of the following statements. Then circle the number that best describes your actions or thoughts, with *1* being "Never" and *10* being "Always."

1. I write clear personal and work goals that guide my achievement.

   1   2   3   4   5   6   7   8   9   10

2. I have developed the skill of picturing my goals clearly in my mind's eye.

   1   2   3   4   5   6   7   8   9   10

3. I believe I can achieve much higher goals than I am now achieving.

   1   2   3   4   5   6   7   8   9   10

4. I feel worthy to achieve higher goals.

   1   2   3   4   5   6   7   8   9   10

5. I frequently review and revise my goals.

   1   2   3   4   5   6   7   8   9   10

6. I break my goals into small steps that I can work on daily.

   1   2   3   4   5   6   7   8   9   10

7. When I set a goal, I always set a specific date to achieve it.

   1   2   3   4   5   6   7   8   9   10

8. My goals are congruent with my values.

   1   2   3   4   5   6   7   8   9   10

9. I view all my goals to be within my possibilities.

   1   2   3   4   5   6   7   8   9   10

10. I'm never in doubt about what my goals and objectives are.

   1   2   3   4   5   6   7   8   9   10

Action Guide: *Daily Success Diary* ✎ ✎

Set Goals

Please score yourself from 1 to 10 for each daily activity, with
1 being "Never" and 10 being "Always."

	S	M	T	W	T	F	S
1. I reviewed my written goals today.							
2. I studied a successful person's actions today.							
3. I focused on the rewards of reaching my goals today.							
4. I thought of my values as I made decisions and interacted with people.							
5. I took time to learn from wise people today.							
Total each day							

12 Invite Customers Back

Cause People to Feel Good
About Their Contact with You

I heard an ad over the radio about a home air-filter device. The ad said it had been used to clean the air at the Pentagon after the 9/11 attack, taking the smoke and fire smell out of the building. I called the toll-free number and talked to one of the nicest, most professional people with whom I've ever visited. Her name was Hannah Lieberman.

Before recommending her filter, she asked me several questions about my home. She asked if I had any allergies. In five to eight minutes she found out quite a bit of information about me. She seemed unusually interested and very genuine, and she made a special effort to be sure that her device was right for me.

She explained the company's money-back guarantee, as well as the product's warranty. I bought the device, and three days later it arrived at my home.

No sooner had I received it than she called me to make sure it had arrived. She asked if I had any questions about the installation, and again explained the return policy and money-back guarantee. She repeated a couple of things she'd learned about my home when I first talked to her.

About two weeks later she called again and asked how I liked the unit. She was so friendly and sincere that rather than being a bother, it was a joy to talk to her. She explained how and when to clean the filter, and said that she would call back when it was time to do that—which she did.

I'm not sure that I've ever had such a pleasant buying experience from anyone. Will I ever purchase anything else from Hannah Lieberman? I don't know, but I would certainly look forward to doing so, because she left me feeling so good about my buying from her. Her attitude exemplified the sixth step in the *G. Val Hi* system: *Invite Customers Back.*

How Do Sales and Service People Leave You Feeling?

I recently had a painting framed at FastFrame. The salesperson was very friendly and helpful in the frame selection. When I picked it up, the frame set the painting off even more than I had anticipated. She pointed out that they had painted a gold strip on one edge of the frame and how it pulled out a similar color in the painting.

I left more than pleased.

A week later I got a thank-you card in the mail containing a $20 gift certificate. It read:

> Thank you for choosing FastFrame as your custom framer. We look forward to seeing you again.

It was signed by Patrick Conrad, the owner of the franchise. The company planted the seeds of positive memories in my mind. It left me feeling very good about my purchase.

Think for a moment about purchase or service experiences

you've had in the last month. What percentage of them left you feeling good about the contact? How often did you leave with a negative feeling?

I went to get a prescription filled last week at the pharmacy counter in my local market and was served by a new person. I handed her the doctor's script form; she looked at it and asked for my date of birth. For a moment her question took me aback. I said, "Charleen never asks me that."

She looked at me as if I had questioned her whole life purpose and shot back, "Well, I'm not Charleen." While saying that, she scanned her eyes over me for a moment, conveying the message, "Don't mess with me, buddy!"

I was reluctant to go back in a couple of hours to pick it up, afraid that I'd be scolded for being so dumb. Being the coward that I am, I was hoping she wouldn't jump on me and shred my self-esteem any more.

The three or four times I've been in the market since then, I've tiptoed by the pharmacy counter, hoping she wouldn't see me. The next time I have a prescription to fill, I'll probably call to see if Charleen is on duty before I do.

Well . . . I am exaggerating a bit, but isn't it interesting how we remember our contacts with people? How seemingly little everyday situations leave us with certain emotions?

Do your customers react the same way?

Last Impressions Are as Important as First Impressions

Here's the key to success with your customers, associates, or other people: *Make sure your* last *impressions are just as impressive as your* first *ones are.*

The Ritz-Carlton Hotels value these two points of contact so much that they list them on the credo cards that each employee carries at all times. Their "Three Steps of Service" are as follows:

1. A warm and sincere greeting. *Use the guest's name, if and when possible.*
2. Anticipation and compliance with guest needs.
3. Fond farewell. *Give them a warm good-bye and use their names, if and when possible.*

Usually, if I'm focused on customers in my greeting and inviting them back, I'll also be tuned in to their other needs in the middle of these two bookends.

Write Your Own *Exit Statements*

In seminars I've conducted, I've asked the participants to write *exit statements.* These are descriptions of how they'd like their customers to describe their contact with them.

How do *you* want people to feel about their contact with you — in person, over the telephone, or even through e-mail? Take a moment to answer these questions.

1. *How do I want people to feel after having contact with me?*
2. *What do I want them to say about me?*
3. *How do I want them to describe their experience with me to others?*

As I ask people to actually write out their answers to these three questions, a transformation often occurs. They have to think in the way their customers might feel, rather than how they themselves feel. This takes the focus off themselves and directs it externally to customers.

People look quizzical when I ask them to write an *exit statement*—they've never thought of doing that before. Then, as they write about how they want their customers to feel and describe them, I see lights coming on in their heads and hear silent gongs going off.

Here's an idea for you. Sit down with three or four of your associates, hand out some index cards, and ask each of them to join you in writing *exit statements*. Ask them to write answers for the three questions that I've just mentioned.

After each of you has written your statements, share yours with your associates, and ask each person to do the same. Challenge them to read their statements each day during the coming week and give special attention to how they end their contacts with either internal associates or external customers. Suggest that they especially evaluate on a scale of 1 to 10—with 1 being "Terrible" and 10 being "Great"—how people with whom they have sales or service experiences leave them feeling. This external observation usually becomes a personal learning experience.

Do the math yourself this next week. After each contact you have with service people, evaluate how they left you feeling.

This will be a great learning experience for you. It can indelibly engrave this simple social action in your automatic responses as you interact with your internal and external customers.

How to Make the Best Last Impressions

Here are three Action Guides to practice this week. Doing them will help you make the best *last impressions* upon people whom you contact—in person, over the telephone, or by e-mail.

1. *Thank them for coming in or contacting you.*
2. *Ask them to return soon.*
3. *Leave them wanting to return.*

Consciously practice these Action Guides, and within 21 to 28 days they'll become automatic habits for you. When they become a part of *who* you are, you'll set yourself apart from most other service providers with whom your customers have contact.

Let's think of each of them.

THANK THEM FOR COMING IN OR CONTACTING YOU

Again, this is a social grace that seems so ordinary it doesn't get much attention from many people. If you don't believe me, go into five stores or shops and tell the person you're just looking. What usually happens is they figure you for a "flake" and leave you to your own wandering. Since they sense that you're not going to add anything to their cash register, you won't get much more attention. Usually when you leave you'll get either a perfunctory "come back" or no response at all.

The words you use to thank customers for coming in or contacting you aren't as important as your actions in focusing your attention on them and causing them to feel good about the visit or contact. Your actions and apparent attitude are what deliver the message.

Not long ago I was in Santa Fe, New Mexico, where our company had its annual convention. The day before it began, I went gallery-hopping. One of the art galleries I visited was the old Fenn Gallery, now owned by Nedra Matteucci. I was greeted in a very friendly way. I asked if I could look around and was invited to do so. I spent thirty to forty minutes enjoying their beautiful works of great painters, such as Frederic Remington, Leon Gaspard, Nicolai Fechin, and the great Southwestern artist Fremont Ellis.

John, the salesperson, invited me to go out to their beautifully landscaped garden to see the incredible array of outdoor sculptures. It was a breathtaking sight. Crab-apple and apricot trees grew around a pond with waterfalls and swans swimming in graceful motions. The 7,000-foot elevation of Santa Fe causes the summer mornings to have a spectacular dazzle. With the brilliance of the morning and the beauty of the gallery, I understood the wonderful feeling of *sensory overload*.

Upon leaving, John positioned himself at the door and said, "I love your shirt." I looked at him to see if he really meant it, and quickly decided he did, which, of course, showed his good taste, because I liked it myself.

He handed me his card and invited me to come in whenever I'm in the city.

What a wonderful experience. His sincerity was a perfect ending to a very enjoyable visit.

I then went to another gallery close by. They had beautiful, very expensive paintings. Two men were at desks inside the entry. They looked up at me when I walked in, but didn't say anything or give me any kind of greeting. They also had some works by the great Russian-turned-Southwest-painter Leon Gaspard. I approached one of the men who were seated at desks and asked the price of one of his paintings. He informed me that I'd have to ask someone else, that it was not in his department. He then pointed to the other man.

When I asked the other person, he looked up the price, told me, and walked off. My feeling was that he didn't think I could afford it.

When I left the gallery, I got no response from either of these two men.

Quite a difference from the Fenn Gallery.

Again, causing people to feel good about contacting you isn't just what you say; it's what you do and who you are. My point is that you can say "thank you" in many ways. You can say it with words or actions. You do it when you stop people for a moment, get their attention, and reconnect with them emotionally.

Reconnecting allows you a moment or two to give psychological value to people, to shut out both of your worlds for just a few seconds and communicate your appreciation to them for entrusting you with a segment of their time.

Don't Be Lulled by the Comings and Goings of People or Events

I know that in the routine of life, where you're having multiple contacts, people become just numbers, and problems become just so many more hassles. I also know that there's a tendency to unconsciously ask, "Is this person or situation going to waste my time?"

For six years I owned a contemporary furniture and interior design business. People came in to look, kill time, or just get out of their houses. Since we could pay our bills only by selling stuff, our natural reaction was to size up people to see if they were just looking or were prospective buyers. Because of the routine and stream of lookers, there was a tendency to not connect with them.

It was a natural habit to develop, and not an easy one to break.

I had an experience one day that taught me a good lesson. A rather plain, coarse-looking person who was about as sensitive and socially engaging as an angry bumble bee came in. Everything I said, she'd challenge me—questioning the truth of my statements.

Part of me wanted to say, "Look, lady, I've got better things to do than allow you to verbally beat me up. Besides, you probably couldn't afford anything I have here, anyway." Fortunately, I kept a thin veil over my desire to give back the treatment she was giving me.

After a while, sensing my thoughts, she said to me, "Young man, I could buy everything you have in this store and pay for it out of my petty cash."

Well, sure enough, I was soon to find out that she could!

As it turned out, she and her husband became loyal customers of ours, spending more money than any other single customer we ever had. They'd been poor, uneducated people. He'd worked in the oilfields of Texas as a roughneck. Through frugality and excellent business sense, they had started an oil-drilling company on a shoestring and had caught the oil boom just right—and the rest was history. They became very wealthy.

My initial impressions were far from correct.

Ask Them to Return Soon

This principle confuses many of the participants in our "The Customer" course, especially ones who are in telesales or teleservice roles, where they may only have one-time contact with customers. Or we have hospital employees who say, "But we can't invite patients back; that'd mean that we want them to get sick again."

I understand their concern, but the point is that *should* they have future health problems, you'd want them to come back to your hospital. Or if their friends or family members need health care, wouldn't you want them to be sent to you?

But we can still miss the point. It's this: Forgetting business—whatever products, services, or problems have been your discussion with customers—wouldn't you want them to have had such a pleasant experience with *you* that they'd want to enjoy *you* again? Like seeds you plant in people's minds that spring up later to bring joy to them, so your leaving them feeling good about your treatment will bring them good future thoughts about you.

A few years ago, at a convention in Seattle, my then business partner, Bernard Petty, bought his wife, Laverne, a ring in a jewelry store in the lobby of the Four Seasons Hotel. Through going in and looking at it several times before making the purchase, Bernard and Laverne struck up such a friendship with the store manager that they invited him and his family to come to Texas and spend a weekend with them.

After purchasing the ring for Laverne, Bernard sent other people into the jewelry store to buy watches. Three summers later, he and his family went back to Seattle. They stayed at the Four Seasons Hotel so they could visit the jewelry store manager, who even talked the hotel into giving the Pettys a suite at the regular room price.

What went on here? What relationship was previously established here? How were good feelings sustained?

Leave Them Wanting to Return

When customer-centered *attitudes* and *values* are shown through your *actions*, customers will cherish good feelings and memories about you. When your attitudes and values are right, your actions will usually be right.

The whole buying, shopping, or service experience plants positive or negative feelings within customers, and this whole experience causes them to have ongoing memories of it.

Once I walked out of a hotel in Minneapolis and saw a hand-printed sign in the window of a cigar store. It said, "No change made!"

Curious, I went in and asked the attendant what the sign meant. Eyeing me suspiciously, he growled through his cigar, "If I didn't have that sign there, people would bother me all day, asking for parking meter change."

"Yeah, well, you certainly wouldn't want that to happen," I thought to myself as I left his shop.

I can still remember thinking, "Hey, man, if I owned that shop I'd put a sign in the window that said, 'Change made with a smile.'"

In fact, as I looked at the small number of parking meters close by, I visualized myself watching them and personally putting a nickel or a dime in them, with a note attached to the driver's wiper blade that said, "When you park close to my store, I'll even try to watch your meter for you. Thanks for referring your friends to me."

This experience became sort of a metaphor for me, and since then I've noticed the same attitude in many businesses. With their actions they clearly say, "No change made here! Don't bother us unless you want to buy something!" Or they say, "And don't ask for any special favors, either!"

Sadly, in these competitive times many of these organizations aren't in business any longer. The ones that are still around will find slimmer chances for survival in the years ahead, as customers demand the high level of service they deserve.

Customers *are* becoming more demanding—which of course they have a right to be. They have more choices as to what and from whom they buy. This presents a gloomy future for some organizations—ones that don't focus on customers' needs. But it spells *insurmountable opportunities* for those wide-awake firms who have shifted to a true customer focus.

One way to cause customers to favorably remember you is to do something that's totally unexpected and out of the ordinary. Simple actions are most memorable—a small, chewy chocolate for your restaurant guest, a genuine "thank you" just before your customer leaves, an inexpensive gift, a thank-you note. Be different; use your imagination.

Businesses that thrive in the future will be the ones that say, "Bother me even if you don't want to buy anything!" Or "Ask me for special favors and just see how fast I give them to you!"

Be creative and send a silent, clear message with your actions: "Change enthusiastically made here!"

What do sales or service people do that causes you to *not* want to return? You may want to notice these actions and even make a list of them. As you list or review them, you can say, "Here are behaviors I don't want to do."

This way you can learn positive lessons from negative experiences.

"Help Me Feel Important!"

Years ago a wise person gave me this advice: "People are going through life with a small sign on their forehead that reads, 'Help me feel important!' "

He went on, "To the extent you remember this need, and take time to fill it with the people you meet, you'll be successful with them."

Good advice!

But let's be honest—we can get so wrapped up in just doing our jobs, or so focused on our own problems or needs, that we don't take time to do this. Or maybe our main focus is our need for others to make us feel important, and we seldom get outside ourselves. This can often happen in our relationships with associates on the job.

My experience in working with people in many organizations reveals a very common problem—not all people get along well with others. Some people demand that their associates bow to them and make them feel important. Their need for recognition or control causes them to become myopic and see only themselves. This almost always causes problems.

Not long ago I was conducting a seminar for dentists and their staff. The first day, after the session was over, a dentist asked if he could visit with me. We sat down for a few minutes while he told me of a challenge he had in his office. His office manager had been with him longer than any other staff person. She was very competent and the patients loved her, and she knew them all.

The problem was that all of his staff disliked her. Staff turnover was higher than he'd have liked it to be. Team spirit was low. This person was difficult to get along with, and demanded that the staff be subservient to her. The more outgoing and attractive they were, the more she seemed to dislike them and treat them badly.

His difficulty was that he knew how she was and the problems she created, but because of her long tenure and knowledge of the patients, he didn't think the office would run without her.

"Have you talked to her?" I asked.

"Several times," he replied. "Things will improve for a week or two, and then problems start up again."

"Are you under the delusion that she might change?" I asked.

His pausing to answer told me that he knew the reality of the situation, but hadn't wanted to deal with it.

"So, what do I do?" he finally asked.

"You know what you have to do, don't you?" I asked.

Again, he paused, finally breathed a sigh, and said, "Yes. I know what I must do."

Four or five months later I got a note from him saying that he'd terminated her and that his office billings had improved over 35 percent.

He said that he couldn't believe how great it was to come to work with such a positive staff as he now had.

Your Work Environment Influences Your Customers' Desire to Return

In Chapter 9 we discussed the power of teamwork as it influences your organization's productivity. Let's take that a step further and think about this positive or negative energy that influences your customers.

In his book *Primal Leadership*, Dan Goleman writes this about the influence of the work environment on customer satisfaction: "There's actually a logarithm that proves that for every 1 percent improvement in the service climate, there's a 2 percent increase in revenue."

These findings certainly emphasize the value of your environment.

Consider the thought that every group of people working together forms a certain degree of energy, and that customers pick up on this. The sum total of people's:

```
  Skills
+ Attitudes
+ Values
+ Cooperative spirit
+ Work environment
= Group energy
```

Let's assume, just for instance, that the previously mentioned dental office had five staff people, which it did. Let's give them these overall attitudinal ratings purely as a way to make a point. Let's assume these ratings are on a scale of +10 to –10, with +10 being the most positive energy and –10 being the most negative energy.

```
    8  Doctor
+   8  Hygienist
+   8  Chair-side assistant
+   8  Receptionist
–   8  Office manager
= 24   Office energy
```

Add 8 + 8 + 8 + 8, and you get 32. Then subtract 8, to get 24. This "for instance" makes the point that one negative person can dull down the whole office's effectiveness. It would be better if she had just been zero—with no positive contributions, or negative ones, either.

Negative people drag down positive people around them. In the dental office's case, replacing the office manager with a new person who had no experience not only replaced a minus 8 attitude, but actually allowed the other people to perform better, because they weren't hampered by the manager's negativity and controlling nature.

Look what happened by removing the negative person and replacing her with a new, inexperienced one.

$$
\begin{array}{rl}
9 & \text{Doctor} \\
+ \ 9 & \text{Hygienist} \\
+ \ 9 & \text{Chair-side assistant} \\
+ \ 9 & \text{Receptionist} \\
+ \ 0 & \text{Office manager} \\
\hline
= 36 & \text{Office energy}
\end{array}
$$

Do the math on this, and you'll see an increase of over 35 percent, as a result of the totals increasing from 24 to 36. Again, these are only numbers to make the point. An actual assessment would be more complete than this.

But back to my main point, that the work environment can often be unconsciously picked up by your customers. We see this in our courses all the time, in situations where customers never see the service people, or have only telephone contacts. Careful observation has led me to believe that not only do customers pick up on individual people's attitudes, but they also seem to intuitively sense the cumulative values, positive attitudes, and team synergy of the organization.

Since we all become a part of the overall service attitudes of the people with whom we work, this means that our own job fulfillment, effectiveness, and enjoyment are all influenced. These internal factors affect your customers' inner feelings about you.

HOW TO GAIN THE MOST FROM THIS CHAPTER

Last impressions are as important as *first* impressions for your ongoing success with customers.

Successful businesses and organizations realize the need to invite customers, guests, or patients back. They know this is a crucial step in causing long-term loyalty and satisfaction.

Becoming adept at inviting people back begins with identifying how you want them to feel after having contact with you.

You can have a powerful impact on your customers when you practice these Action Guides.

1. *Thank them for coming in or contacting you.*
2. *Ask them to return soon.*
3. *Leave them wanting to return.*

I strongly recommend that you design your own *exit statement.* This is a written statement of how you want customers to describe their experiences with you. It will give you a focus that has a positive influence on your attitudes and actions when dealing with people.

Remember the importance of *last* impressions, and make sure the last one *you* make on people is strong and positive. They will be far more likely to contact you again or refer their friends to you.

People go where they're appreciated—where they feel welcome and valued. And they return to offices, businesses, or organizations where they're invited back.

Always take time to ensure that your customers will feel they've had a special experience with you.

Self-Assessment: *Invite Customers Back*

Take a moment to read each of the following statements. Then circle the number that best describes your actions or thoughts, with *1* being "Never" and *10* being "Always."

1. I make sure at the end of each contact that people know I value them.

   1   2   3   4   5   6   7   8   9   10

2. I have written a clearly defined *exit statement*.

   1   2   3   4   5   6   7   8   9   10

3. I review my *exit statement* daily.

   1   2   3   4   5   6   7   8   9   10

4. I want customers to think of me whenever they have future needs that I can help them fill.

   1   2   3   4   5   6   7   8   9   10

5. I pay as much attention to people who don't buy from me as ones who do.

   1   2   3   4   5   6   7   8   9   10

6. I consciously contribute to our team's overall positive attitude toward customers.

   1   2   3   4   5   6   7   8   9   10

7. I consciously contribute to our team's overall synergy.

   1   2   3   4   5   6   7   8   9   10

8. I carefully guard against taking customers for granted.

   1   2   3   4   5   6   7   8   9   10

9. I always notice people as *people*, not just as numbers coming and going.

   1   2   3   4   5   6   7   8   9   10

10. I have a longer-term view of customer relationships than just their single contacts.

    1   2   3   4   5   6   7   8   9   10

Action Guide: *Daily Success Diary*

Invite Customers Back

Please score yourself from 1 to 10 for each daily activity, with *1* being "Never" and *10* being "Always."

	S	M	T	W	T	F	S
1. I thanked each person for his or her contact today.							
2. I took a special moment to focus on customers as people.							
3. I wanted each person to feel valued.							
4. I wanted each person to want to have contact with me again.							
5. I consciously remembered to apply my *exit statement* with each person.							
Total each day							

Afterword

There are a few fundamental rules of life. When truth, honesty, uprightness, and sincerity—integrity—are practiced in our daily behaviors, they lead to sustained success and emotional well-being. Stress, emotional clutter, and even eventual failure result when these rules are compromised.

In the invisible scheme of things this truth is carried out— *Great is the person or organization who helps the most people enjoy the most benefits.*

Herein lies the secret to the personal happiness, self-respect, and fulfillment you deserve to enjoy. It will bring true career and personal success.

Bless you in your quest for these.

About the Author

Ron Willingham is founder and CEO of Integrity Systems, Inc., an international training and development company, with more than 1.5 million graduates in eighty nations. His organization is the leader in helping organizations succeed with ethical, values-driven people development strategies. Integrity Systems' client list reads like a Who's Who in business: Johnson & Johnson, American Red Cross, IBM, the Principal Financial Group, the Guardian Life Insurance Company, the Library of Congress, Franklin Templeton, and more than 2,000 others. He is the author of *Integrity Selling for the 21st Century*, as well as eight other books. More than 26,000 facilitators have been certified to conduct his courses.

For information about his courses you may go to www.integrity systems.com.